HOW TO SAY GOODBYE TO YOUR COMFORT ZONE

HACKNEY AND JONES

Copyright © 2021 by Hackney And Jones

All rights reserved.

No part of this book may be reproduced in any form or by any electronic or mechanical means, including information storage and retrieval systems, without written permission from the author, except for the use of brief quotations in a book review.

Claim Your Freebie NOW!

Get Good At Problem Solving

Want to know the secret behind getting good at problem solving? Everyone seems to be able to do it, but you're stuck in the pile of endless to-do lists with little progress.

Ok, so how do I get my FREE book?

EASY! See the next page

Claim Your Freebie NOW

Instructions:

1. Open the camera or the QR reader application on your smartphone.
2. Point your camera at the QR code to scan the QR code.
3. A notification will pop-up on screen.
4. Click on the notification to open the website link

Claim Your Freebie NOW

Instructions

1. Open the camera/the QR code application on your smartphone.
2. Point your camera at the QR code to scan the QR code.
3. A notification will pop up on screen.
4. Click on the notification to go to the website link.

SCAN ME

Contents

Introduction	ix
1. What Exactly Is The Comfort Zone	1
2. Examples Of A Comfort Zone - Determining Your Comfort Zone Level	4
3. Is Your Comfort Zone A Bad Place?	21
4. Why Don't I Feel I Can Leave My Comfort Zone?	24
5. How Can I Come Out Of My Comfort Zone Daily?	30
6. Fun Ways To Leave Your Comfort Zone	39
7. The Art Of Self-Questioning	47
8. Change Your Focus	49
9. Getting What You Want	55
10. Making Your Life GREAT	61
11. Other Elements In Determining Drive And Direction	65
12. Goals With Purpose	72
13. Getting Outside Your Comfort Zone Under Any Circumstances	76
14. How Can I Get Outside My Comfort Zone In My Relationships?	79
15. Fail Hard But Learn Fast	84
16. The Surprising Power of Visualisation	88
17. Adjust Your Locus Of Control	92
18. Your Decision-Making Method	96
19. The Value Of Ignoring	101
20. The Perfectionism Devil	105
Afterword	111
Feedback	113

Introduction

In a fairyland, no one would have to stretch beyond their comfort zone to thrive at work, and all the responsibilities and tasks we need to execute would match perfectly with our personalities. But regrettably, this is not usually the case. Conflict-avoidant managers generally need to embrace conflict—or at least learn to endure it. Timid entrepreneurs need to be able to propose and promote themselves and their ideas. Introverts need to network. Self-conscious executives need to produce speeches; people-pleasers need to convey unpleasant news.

We've all read about the renowned innovators, scientists, and designers whose discoveries transformed the world forever. And, based on the stories, many of their brilliant insights seemed predestined: James Watt got the idea for the steam engine while watching his mother's tea kettle boil on the stove; Alexander Fleming discovered penicillin after leaving a petri dish open all night; we all remember Sir Isaac Newton's apple legend.

Whatever led to each of those pivotal moments, throughout centuries, we have created certain assumptions about the men and women whose creativity still inspires us today. Although their biographies reveal incredible work ethic and perseverance, we thought they were also born with a unique set of skills that permitted them to see common things from a different perspective.

This kind of genius, we were informed, was gifted to a select few. You either had it, or you didn't. For a very long time, this common thinking went unquestioned. Children were divided into distinct ability groups based on standardised examinations conducted in elementary school, which were generally used throughout their academic careers. We assumed we didn't have creative talent if no one had noticed it in us by high school. We were urged to work hard and pay our dues once we started a career choice, and then success—at whatever level we were destined for—would follow.

But what if genius isn't like that? What if Einstein and Edison were merely utilising their minds differently than we do? "Bare lists of words are found indicative to an imaginative and agitated mind," Ralph Waldo Emerson reportedly said of the creative process. This implies that creativity is a state of mind rather than an intrinsic aptitude. What if ingenuity isn't so much given as it is awakened?

We're frequently faced with situations where we need to adapt and alter our behaviour as we develop, learn, and improve in our jobs and careers. It's simply a fact of life in the modern world. Without the ability—and the courage—to take the risk, we risk missing out on critical possibilities for improvement. We may also neglect to complete duties that are necessary for the advancement of our enterprises and careers. This is where this book comes into effect. The purpose of this book is to provide you with the knowledge and tools—as well as the courage—to take that leap, to go outside your comfort zone, and to do so in a way that is both authentic and productive, accomplishing the goals you set for yourself while not losing yourself in the process.

Suppose you've ever been interested in the issue of comfort zones and are familiar with Google's search feature.

You're likely to come across several pictures and diagrams. You have bold goldfish leaping from one fishbowl to the next. People are walking on tightropes, parachuting, and jumping off cliffs, telling you that "everything you've always wanted is one step beyond your comfort zone" and that "you're only confined by the walls you build for yourself." And then there are the stories—successful and confident people who dared to go for it, and take a leap, and are now spokespeople for Comfort Zone, Inc imploring us to do the same: The only thing to be afraid of is fear!

How do you get from one location to another? It's wonderful to imagine it's as simple as a fish hopping from one bowl to the next, but it's not the case. Stretching beyond your comfort zone necessitates a significant amount of effort and time. You'll need motivation. Motivation, on the other hand, isn't enough to close the deal. What's really needed is a clear road map for getting from a position of fear, paralysis, and avoidance to a place where you're willing and able to take that leap and begin a more positive cycle of learning and development.

When we are forced to behave outside of our comfort zones, we frequently feel overwhelmed and despairing. However, the reality is that we are confronted with a series of extremely predictable and identifiable obstacles, which we may solve by following the rules presented in this book. This book will explain why acting outside your comfort zone is so difficult and will guide you in developing the confidence and ability to flex your behaviour successfully. The structure presented in the book is not one-size-fits-all; rather, it is tailored and customised to the specific issues you face in every situation.

So, why did we write this book? We realised that being scared to come out of your comfort zone was actually a very common issue with a range of different people. We conducted some research on Twitter, asking questions to see which answers people voted for. The results are below:

Q1. What stops you from leaving your comfort zone?

- Fear of the unknown - 29%
- Social construct - 8%
- Laziness (be honest) - 46%
- Don't feel the need - 17%

Q2. When you know somebody regularly seeks things outside their comfort zone, do you think:

- It's a positive thing - 84%
- It's reckless - 16%

Q3. Do you feel like you never leave your comfort zone?

- Yes - 42%
- No - 58%

Q4. Say you wanted to start leaving your comfort zone, what's stopping you right now?

- Don't know where to start - 26%
- Fear - 44%
- Will it be worth it? - 30%
- Family/friends response - 0%

Q5. Would you love to start leaving your comfort zone more and more?

- Yes - 72%
- No - 28%

Let's consider the answers to the last two questions. The most popular response to question 4 was **fear** being the reason not to leave the comfort zone. In question 5, 72% of respondents decided they **would** like to leave their comfort zone.

So read on, and let's discover together what the comfort zone is and work towards identifying how we say goodbye to it.

What Exactly Is The Comfort Zone

CHALLENGES FORCE you to learn things about yourself that you didn't know before. They're what makes the instrument stretch, and they're what pushes you to do things you wouldn't normally do.

If you want to continue growing, developing, and remaining healthy as you get older, you must step outside of your comfort zone. "Use it or lose it" used to be enough, but a new study suggests that to battle ageing diseases, we must keep our brains and bodies active and learn new things regularly. By stepping outside of your comfort zone, you can live a longer, healthier, and more fulfilling life.

On the other hand, many others will go to any length to remain in their comfort zones. It is believed that many people never travel more than 50 miles from their hometown, and only about a quarter of Americans have a passport. Travelling is only one of many ways to push yourself outside of your comfort zone. It's not so much what you do as it is that you actually do something to develop yourself.

You will feel lively and full of new energy after going out of your comfort zone. The more you take risks, the more confident and capable you become.

. . .

YOUR COMFORT ZONE is comprised of 4 distinct areas:

- You may be out of your comfort zone if you are in a place or setting where you have never been before. Travelling, placing yourself in new settings, attending networking meetings, and appreciating other physical environments are all ways to grow and learn.
- Travelling and immersing yourself in a new environment for a day, a week, a month, or a year may be a freeing and life-changing experience.
- People - Go to a lecture, a networking meeting, travel, volunteer, attend a class, or attend a party to meet and engage with people you don't know.
- Pursuits - You are in your comfort zone if you continue to engage in activities that you are comfortable with and skilled at. You step out of your comfort zone when you begin a new sport, skill, or activity that you are unfamiliar with.

We would frequently travel to new cities and villages to experience the countryside as a family. These trips pushed us out of our comfort zones and into new territory. From reading the map to picking where to have lunch or go for a hike, our senses were all on high alert. Travelling a long distance is exciting, yet we found driving 60 kilometres to a new village or region equally exhilarating.

THE BRAIN'S POWER: Completing tasks that you're comfortable with puts you in your comfort zone while stretching yourself to try a new skill or task that pushes you out.

Our brains are always being challenged as we discover new social marketing technologies. We've concluded that we won't be able to learn them all at once, but one new one per month until we feel comfortable seems like a decent pace to keep us improving.

Why don't we step outside our comfort zones more often?

In essence, we are still operating on old primate instincts that tell us to keep safe, stick with the herd, and protect ourselves from potential danger. This was once crucial, but it is no longer relevant.

2

Examples Of A Comfort Zone - Determining Your Comfort Zone Level

EVEN THOUGH WE all have varied comfort zones for different reasons, one thing is certain: we all have them, whether they are related to the most acute fears and anxieties, deeply buried restrictions, or outright strange phobias. This book is all about supporting you in stepping out of your particular comfort zone and letting go of the fears, anxieties, and limits that come with it. Pushing boundaries and going above and beyond to master a new level of thinking that will allow you to live the life you truly desire!

So, before we get started, it'll be helpful to complete the Zone Test to determine your present comfort zone and identify what areas of your life are holding you back, from the obvious to the things you may not be aware of. This will provide you with a personal platform from which to work and a higher sense of self-awareness from which to grow.

You'll be able to see which zone you fall into and look at the areas of your life where you may positively think differently and alter to drive yourself forward to zone zero by taking this introspective quiz. This is the point at which you have no more restrictions or illogical concerns, only obstacles that you know you can easily overcome as and when they arise, allowing you to live a fulfilling and exhilarating existence.

It's important to note that there are no right or wrong answers to the following questions; instead, these indicate how much you exhibit the common psychological traits associated with pushing personal boundaries and stepping outside common comfort zones to live your life to the fullest and achieve everything you want.

You can also read more about the meanings of each question and response. This should be done after you've finished the test so that it doesn't affect your answers. It will assist you to comprehend your responses better and understand your existing inner self, allowing you to get the most out of this book.

You'll get the most out of this test if you answer the questions as honestly and fast as possible because it's a measurement tool for you and your personal development.

Because these questions are generic and based on self-analysis, the answers should not be interpreted as a formal psychological test but rather as an indication of your present comfort zone and zone description at this point in your life.

The Zone Test

Choose the option that best fits your needs.

Q1. For personal growth, the last time I did something that terrified me or made a brave decision was:

1. I can't seem to recall anything.
2. In the previous month.
3. Within the last 12 months.
4. In the last six months.

Q2. If I find myself in a circumstance where I have the option of doing something that makes me feel uncomfortable, I will:

1. Completely avoid the situation.
2. I pushed myself forward on purpose.
3. Make up an excuse to avoid doing something I don't want to do.
4. Decide that if it is necessary, I will do it.

Q3. I have total trust in my instincts:

1. Rarely.
2. Always.
3. Occasionally.
4. Usually.

Q4. Others think of me as unusual or out of the ordinary:

1. Never.
2. Always.
3. Perhaps.
4. Usually.

Q5. Making changes is difficult for me:

1. Always.
2. Never.
3. Usually.
4. Occasionally.

Q6. Scenario: I'm the CEO of a company, and I'm faced with the difficult task of deciding which of two employees to fire. One is my sibling, who is competent but not outstanding at work, yet I am aware that their circumstances make them utterly reliant on their job. The other person is indeed a genius at their job and has a flawless work history.

I'd go with the family member:

1. Always.
2. Occasionally.
3. Usually.
4. Never.

Q7. When there's a difficulty, I stay calm and see a lot of options:

1. Never.
2. Always.
3. Occasionally.
4. Usually.

Q8. Someone has to be in charge of a given project, so the person with the most knowledge should take the lead, even if that person isn't me:

1. Never.
2. Usually.
3. Occasionally.
4. Always.

Q9. In my life, I am certain that I have all I require to care for myself completely; I think that I am always accountable for everything that occurs in my life, even if it is not my fault:

1. Never.
2. Always.
3. Occasionally.
4. Usually.

Q10. I update my profile picture on social media platforms like WhatsApp, Facebook, Twitter, and Instagram:

1. Very often.
2. Occasionally.
3. Quite frequently.
4. Never.

Q11. I'm now doing everything I can to live the life I want, regardless of barriers or challenges:

1. Never.
2. Always.
3. Occasionally.
4. Usually.

Q12. Open-ended (non-specific) plans that fit inside a general framework don't bother me:

1. Never.
2. Always.
3. Occasionally.
4. Usually.

Q13. I do what I do because I have to, and I don't see any other options:

1. Always.
2. Never.
3. Occasionally.
4. Usually.

Q14. I have previously participated in some of the following sports/activities: skydiving, bungee jumping, scuba/shark diving, paragliding, flying/piloting yourself, climbing a mountain or volcano, paint balling, motor racing, speedboating, skiing, large theme park rides/roller coasters, or similar:

1. Never.
2. Yes, and I do it whenever I can.
3. I'm simply not interested.
4. I tried, but I'll never do it again.

Q15. If I truly desire something in life, I will always find a way to achieve it. I've set some objectives for myself, and I'm confident that I'll reach them:

1. Never.
2. Always.

3. Occasionally.
4. Usually.

Q16. I can't begin new tasks for which I believe I lack experience, qualifications, or funding:

1. Always.
2. Never.
3. Usually.
4. Occasionally.

Q17. I have severe anxiety, fear, or phobia that stops me from doing or being able to accomplish the following things:

1. True.
2. In the past and overcome.
3. Sometimes.
4. Never.

Q18. I dislike being around indecisive folks:

1. This is quite true.
2. True, but on rare occasions.
3. Usually true.
4. False.

Q19. I enjoy going to areas I've never visited before:

1. Never.
2. Always.
3. Occasionally.
4. Usually.

Q20. Lack of regularity, unusual settings, and doing things I don't generally do make me feel uncomfortable:

1. Always.
2. Never.
3. Occasionally.
4. Usually.

Q21. I play games and sports for enjoyment and fitness, not for the sole purpose of winning (except professional sports):

1. Never.
2. Always.
3. Occasionally.
4. Usually.

Q22. I'm not going to try anything new or say anything that hasn't been said before:

1. Always.
2. Never.
3. Usually.
4. Occasionally.

Q23. If I have a problem with something that has to be addressed, I address it as soon as possible:

1. Never.
2. Always.
3. Occasionally.
4. Usually.

Q24. It doesn't stop me from responding even though I don't always know the answer for sure; I say what I think is best and go on:

1. Never.
2. Always.
3. Occasionally.
4. Usually.

Q25. I won't do these activities if I'm afraid of embarrassing myself:

1. Always.
2. Never.
3. Usually.
4. Occasionally.

CHOOSE true or false for the following statements.

Q26. If my doctor strongly advises me or simply thinks that I will take their opinion on a crucial topic, but I disagree, I am adamant in going with my own decision:

- True.
- False.

Q27. I don't generally worry over my mistakes:

- True.
- False.

Q28. Suppose there's something I want/need, like starting a business or charity, having children, going on a personal mission, moving abroad, changing or starting a new job or career, getting more education/qualifications, writing a book, surgery, treatment, therapy, or anything else. In that case, I never find an excuse to put it off:

- True.
- False.

Q29. My purpose, which was profound and life-changing, was completed:

- True.
- False.

Q30. When anything has to be accomplished under time constraints, I usually don't mind and thrive under pressure:

- True.
- False.

Q31. I am confident in my abilities and in who I am. Regardless of what others think of me, I don't need to justify myself:

- True.
- False.

THE ANSWERS and Zones

Points for your answers to questions 1 to 25:
a = 1 point.
b = 4 points.
c = 2 points.
d = 3 points.

POINTS for your answers to questions 26 to 31:
True = 2 points.
False = 1 point.

HERE's a quick rundown of what each question is about:

Q1. Personal limits and general personality/life direction.

. . .

Q2. Self-motivation to push oneself and put oneself in a position to succeed.

Q3. Self-awareness, self-consciousness, confidence, and self-reliance are all aspects of self-awareness.

Q4. Self-confidence, awareness, and thinking style.

Q5. Change resistance and flexibility.

Q6. Emotional reasoning and the need to be liked are two factors that influence our decisions.

Q7. Pressure, confidence, problem-solving, and flexible/creative thinking.

Q8. Control, pride, and results-oriented pragmatism.

Q9. Self-reliance, resourcefulness, confidence, and independence; a desire for clarity.

Q10. Seeking social approval - the need for recognition, to be liked, to fit in with the popular culture, personal fears, comparison/competition with others to be "good enough"/need to assert.

Q11. Ambition and a focus on solutions rather than issues.

. . .

Q12. Flexibility, self-confidence, and trust in life's process.

Q13. Taking advantage of a situation, acting out of necessity or possibility, determination, and subjection.

Q14. Enjoying the rush of excitement and seeking thrills.

Q15. Determination, foreknowledge of the future, and the power of a positive belief system.

Q16. Fear of making mistakes or losing.

Q17. Existing fear assessment methods.

Q18. Taking command and maintaining control.

Q19. Dealing with uncertainty and adventure.

Q20. Fear of the unknown, as well as a need for stability and safety.

Q21. Fear of shame and failure – capacity to perceive the broader picture.

. . .

Q22. Control and experimentation.

Q23. Courage and assertiveness.

Q24. Fear of making mistakes and independent thought.

Q25. Inhibitions.

Q26. Authority, independent thought, self-belief, and self-assurance are all important qualities to have.

Q27. Self-assurance, anxiety levels, and decision-making are all factors to consider.

Q28. Fears that aren't conscious.

Q29. Expectations and current situation.

Q30. Putting pressure on oneself and one's way of thinking.

Q31. Judgment.

ZONE TEST SCORES

THE COMFY ZONE (<50)

You want to stay in your comfort zone: you're more likely to avoid risk, be afraid of making mistakes and taking risks, and be reluctant to change. When it comes to pushing boundaries, you're more cautious and apprehensive, preferring to play it safe and content rather than risking more; as a result, you settle for less. Perhaps you've been waiting for the proper moment to change how you feel, and now is the time to unleash a transformed, forward-focused you who believes you now deserve all you've only ever dreamed about. If one person can accomplish it, so can you, and this book will provide you with the tools, mindset, and practical resources you need to succeed. You may now turn your dreams into a practical plan.

THE EXPLORING ZONE (51–74)

You're probably getting ready to take action, hoping to build confidence and let go of fears, judgments, and emotional reasoning, perhaps with an image in mind of the person you'd like to be or the life you'd like to live. You appear to have a fair amount of concerns and anxieties, but you're mainly conscious of them and wish to get rid of them. The main thing you need to do is let go of inhibitions and the desire to be in charge. You enjoy gently pushing yourself and trying new things, but only in a safe environment to reduce danger and the likelihood of making mistakes or failing. The resilience-builders will be a big aid and a big step forward in helping you transition through zones and get to where you want to go.

THE BREAK-OUT ZONE (75–100)

You are already breaking out. Manifesting or feeling prepared for new levels of thinking and that final push to zone zero. You have all of the characteristics of a zone-zero personality, but you need to be more congruent and consistent in them, with complete conviction and unwavering self-belief.

You are unquestionably a risk-taker who thrives on a good challenge. You are generally unafraid of failure or making mistakes; nevertheless, apprehension and self-doubt can occasionally prevent you from truly going for it and taking advantage of more possibilities with a good chance of success. Learning to trust the process of life, as well as oneself, would be beneficial. It will also help if you improve your intuition even further. You are unconcerned by other people's opinions, but you are well aware of them, which might sometimes cause you to stutter in your personal development.

In general, you are a daring, thrill-seeking individual who is not afraid to stand out. You are often risk-averse and enjoy pushing yourself outside of your comfort zone. The book's concluding chapters, in particular, will be invaluable in giving you that final push.

Zone Zero (101 +)

You're already there, so congrats! Perhaps you're looking for some reminders of who you truly are if you're feeling off-kilter for any reason? Otherwise, you wouldn't have taken the test or found it in the first place (whether consciously or subconsciously, and through whatever improbable method - you'll know why!).

This occurs to everyone, and you'll find everything you need in this book, whether it's positive encouragement to rekindle your flame or a stimulus to push you to the next level.

When transitioning between levels, no matter where you are in terms of your present comfort zone, there is always an uncomfortable and boundary-pushing period that we must all push through and conquer. This is the period where actual positive transformation occurs, helping us to grow and progress to new heights. This growth builds our evolution, and it is at this stage, we truly learn and transition into who and what we eventually want to be to achieve complete fulfilment. It's also a good idea to ask yourself the following questions:

Noting down why you supplied the answers you did and what you were explicitly referring to can make for a more interesting contrast when evaluating your progress.

Finally, did you learn anything new about yourself as a result of pondering the questions?

Are you ready to push your comfort zone to the edge, learn more about yourself, or simply spark a new fresh purpose to keep things interesting and test how far you can go with no bounds and no thinking?

3

Is Your Comfort Zone A Bad Place?

As we grow older and progress through life, we develop habits, customs, and routines. We settle into a routine that is convenient, manageable, and acceptable to others around us. However, the majority of us yearn for more. A better career, a better social life, a better house, a car, and holidays are all things we wish for. We have this nagging feeling that we could be better than we are, but we disregard it. We believe that where we are now is where we are supposed to be and that all those who keep telling us that we can do better and achieve greater things are just snake oil salespeople attempting to sell us something.

Thousands of people have gotten off the couch and started going for a run every evening, read self-help books, attended courses and workshops, and decided to transform their lives and achieve great things due to this thinking. People like you and me have altered our lives and achieved success because the desire to be better than they were was too strong to ignore, and they stepped out of their comfort zones. They disregarded the doubters and so-called friends who chastised them for their failure to push themselves beyond their comfort zones.

Every day, we all have the chance to make a difference in

our lives. We always have the option of breaking our detrimental habits and routines and replacing them with more positive, life-improving activities. If you've gained weight over the years due to your fast food addiction, you can choose to stop eating junk food. You have the option of eating healthily. Every day, you can opt to get off the couch and go for a one-hour stroll. If you don't like your current career, you can always enrol in a local college to gain new skills and find a new one. If you're having trouble paying your mortgage and are falling deeper into debt, you can always take on a part-time job to boost your income. Rather than sitting at home complaining about how little money you have, you could sit down and create an online course that you can sell.

There are many ways to modify and enhance your life; all you have to do is recognise that your existing habits and routines aren't serving you well and decide to change them.

None of this is simple. What, on the other hand, is the alternative? What will happen if you continue to live a self-destructive, unpleasant lifestyle? One thing is certain: it will not be easy.

It's all too tempting to stay in our comfort zones and blame outside influences for how our lives have turned out. External forces are unconcerned. The government is unconcerned if you chose to kill yourself by sitting on the couch every night eating fast food. The government is most likely ecstatic that you're doing it. It implies you'll have less money to save for retirement. You can change the course of your life no matter where you are right now. It only takes one decision to let go of what is holding you back and begin taking steps toward the life you deserve and can create for yourself. It's entirely up to you.

Thousands of people, just like you and me, make decisions every day to step outside of their comfort zones and improve their lives. They succeed on occasion and fail on occasion. That's just the way things go in life. However, stepping beyond their comfort zones makes people stronger, more driven to improve, and their lives gradually improve. They become more optimistic, less accepting of life as it is, and they continue to progress. The benefit of opting to step beyond your comfort zone is that it demonstrates that everything is possible, and you gain momentum toward becoming a better, stronger, and happier version of yourself.

Your safe haven is a dangerous place to be. It keeps you from growing, from doing all that you can, and it makes you unhappy.

4

Why Don't I Feel I Can Leave My Comfort Zone?

ACTING outside of your comfort zone is challenging, but it's difficult for a variety of reasons. You'll be more equipped to deal with these issues once you understand them.

We've identified five major psychological roadblocks that people experience when attempting to act outside of their comfort zones.

The authenticity difficulty: the feeling that "This isn't me at all," as well as the distress that comes with it.

The likeability challenge: the fear that doing so will make people dislike me and the anxiety that comes with it.

The competency challenge: the realisation that "I'm not very good at this conduct, and it's clear to others," accompanied by feelings of embarrassment and, maybe, shame.

The resentment challenge: the overwhelming sensation that I "shouldn't have to be doing this activity" in the first place, as well as the irritation and anger that comes with it.

The morality issue: the sense that the action isn't something I "should be doing," as well as the anxiety and guilt that can accompany it.

. . .

You won't always face all five of these difficulties every time you step out of your comfort zone. But, in reality, any one of these obstacles could be enough to make this extremely difficult. We'll get into the creative strategies we come up with to avoid acting outside our comfort zones (in part to avoid these feelings), but first, let's look at the obstacles themselves—why it's so difficult for us to step outside our comfort zones in the first place.

As you can see, acting outside your comfort zone can be a difficult endeavour, whether it's due to a stylistic or morals difficulty, or probably both. People may feel inauthentic, incompetent, resentful, fearful that others will not like this new version of themselves, and afraid that what they're doing violates their moral standards.

And the variety of feelings that arise from these events is wide: from anxiety and distress to frustration and remorse. Of course, people do not always encounter all of this in a single situation, though possible. However, even one or two of these emotions might be disturbing. You don't need anyone to tell you what the outcome could be. Let say that it's not always what you're hoping for.

Paralysis is one of the possible outcomes. You've been overpowered with emotion to the point where you can't act or think straight.

In our research, we discovered that crying is a more common reaction than you might think. People are sometimes hesitant to leave their comfort zones because they know they will cry—or they fear they'll cry. There are times when it just bursts forth uncontrollably. That was the situation, for example, with a Fortune 500 company's vice president of human resources. She hurried into her immediate supervisor's office and burst into tears after feeling slighted during a meeting with her director. The slight in this case wasn't a one-time experience; it was a collection of feelings accumulated over time due to being slighted several times and never have the bravery to address her director about her feelings.

The reactions you just read were very intense when you were forced to behave outside of your comfort zone. However, emotions do not have to be that strong to be disruptive. There are some cases where people's emotions, when confronted with a situation outside of their comfort zones, are just disruptive or uncomfortable enough to shift their mindset from "approach" to "avoid"—from being willing to take a chance on dealing with an uncomfortable situation to doing everything they can to avoid it. And it's this incredible ability we all have to avoid circumstances outside of our comfort zones that we'll be focusing on next.

Fear

Many behavioural psychologists and other healthcare specialists will gladly tell you that there are no magic words that can be stated to make us feel less anxious, uneasy, or afraid. They believe that the only way to overcome these sentiments is to change our behaviour, which is why they advocate for the "Screw it, just do it" or "Do Something Every Day That Scares Your" mentality. In a nutshell, they argue that the only way to overcome an anxious sensation or a deep fear is to address it – which, of course, involves learning to deal with what makes us uncomfortable, which will unavoidably push us out of our comfort zone.

To be sure, all of this is true, but only to a point; if it were that simple, wouldn't we all face our anxieties and be done with it?

We must first change how we think before we can change how we feel because it is the thinking part that contains all of the specific neuro-chemicals and pathways that initially cause irrational fear; it is the subsequent feeling or emotion that changes how we behave and, as a result, the outcomes we achieve.

So, some really strong words and actions can help you release unneeded pre-anxiety; you may need to address this first before tackling your principal fear and making significant good changes.

After all, everything that comes with stepping outside your comfort zone and breaking boundaries inevitably include establishing an exciting new reality. A new you who attracts radically different results, and such change can be just as frightening as facing the initial fear for some people.

As a result, taking the strategy of using resilience-builders and root-cause tactics first will enable you to notice and act on your anxieties, remove limits, and break your comfort zone in the first place. Rather than using these strategies to conquer your fear in a reactive sense, this will develop your ability to address your fear by looking back on how you successfully fought it.

When you're ready to put it to the test, what was once a difficulty and an overwhelming worry will be nothing more than a memory. This is what we call a "genuine" problem blowout.

Dᴜᴅ you know that when it comes to some universal anxieties - for example:

- **Aerophobia** is the fear of flying. A plane crash is less likely than becoming a professional athlete or being involved in a car accident.
- **Astraphobia** is the fear of thunder and lightning. Thunder isn't considered very dangerous, and being struck by lightning is extremely rare, as up to 90% of lightning travels from cloud to cloud rather than reaching the ground.
- **Arachnophobia** is the fear of spiders. Only 12 spider species out of 40,000 are capable of causing major injury to humans.
- **Dentophobia** is the fear of going to the dentist. Many traumatic dental treatments have been

superseded by modern dentistry techniques such as air abrasion.

Not to add, if you're worried about some things hurting you - you'll learn new scientific quantum ways of thinking later in the book that will help you avoid this.

WE ARE BORN with only two "real" fears: the fear of falling (sometimes confused with the fear of heights) and the fear of loud noises. That is to say, anything else we are afraid of is a fiction we have made up and are clinging to in our imaginations.

Fears are thus merely stories we make ourselves, and they can be categorised as False Evidence Appearing Real.

As a result, one of the guiding ideas here is to assist you in developing resilience and dealing with anything that terrifies you - large or small, anything that holds you back in life. It will help you in identifying the source of your fear and removing it for good.

It will force you to think carefully about your life and push your boundaries by forcing you to leave your comfort zone.

How simple is it to go through life content with being comfortable and toasty in one's comfort zone?

Comfort zones, on the other hand, can create a boring monotony that prevents us from growing and developing personally, socially, and professionally; we could be achieving goals we once thought were possible, but if we stay too comfortable, we accept them dwindling or, even worse, we simply give up on them.

Following the process of gradually stepping out of your comfort zone will assist you in viewing life in a new way; as a more exciting adventure. So much so that when you adjust your perspective on life, you will discover a whole new world.

In essence, you'll be deciding to take control of your mind and, therefore, your life. Instead of letting the outside world determine how you feel on the inside, which all too often becomes a self-defeating vicious circle, you'll start to determine your internal reality, which will then change your external reality – how you experience the world and how life treats you in response; basically, the results you get. The moment we all decide to take full responsibility for ourselves and recognise and accept that we are the only ones who can influence where we want to go in life, we will have made the most significant change! As a result, the goal of this book is to show you how to do it so that the concept of a comfort zone will soon be outdated.

Working through this process can help you develop resilience, so you won't be afraid to explore new frontiers or address things you were previously afraid of, such as fear of the unknown, fear of failure, or fear of change.

All too often, it takes something extremely traumatic in a person's life for them to understand their need, or even desire, to change. You won't have to wait for this to happen if you use all of the techniques in this book. You can begin by taking tiny efforts today to achieve large strides and substantial positive changes, later on accomplishing everything you wish.

By thinking about it, you can make a single change in an instant. Things will look different if you begin to perceive things differently, and you will soon feel like a completely new person.

Fear is often an ethereal product of our ideas, which is the most exciting element of this insight! We might go even further and conclude that fear is only a reaction to the situation. The only genuine issue is a manifestation of our ideas linked to the trigger.

So, if one individual can be fearless about something that scares the living daylights out of you... you can lose any fear by adopting the appropriate mindset!

5

How Can I Come Out Of My Comfort Zone Daily?

POSITIVE THINKING alone will not make your life ideal. Some people believe that once they start thinking positively, everything will be rainbows and ponies. No. You'll still have daily problems, but your mindset will change, and that's the true difference.

Those self-assured appear to be insecure individuals to be fantastic because they appear to overcome all of life's challenges with ease and a smile on their faces. It's a chicken-and-egg situation: self-confidence breeds positivity because you know you can succeed, and positivity breeds belief.

Being appreciative and having an "I can do it" mindset are good thoughts to actively keep in your mind and in your daily routine to stop the negative small talk in your head. Humans have a strong addiction to habits. We all have habits, and we can't help ourselves from doing certain things in the same way over and over again. So let's take advantage of this fundamental quality and use it to our advantage.

Let us get addicted to good habits, replacing bad habits with good ones and destructive habits with constructive ones. What are these bad habits, exactly?

Start your day with a pleasant idea when you wake up. Pin it next to your bed to serve as a reminder until you no longer need it because it has become a habit. Don't dread Mondays or mornings—enjoy the fact that you have another day ahead of you to learn, love, and be joyful.

Quit complaining about it! Ignore your Pavlovian response, and don't do it when you go out of your house and encounter the neighbour with whom you always share your grievances about negative things that happen to you. Instead, welcome your neighbour with a cheerful greeting and remark on how wonderful the day is. Talk about the positive aspects of your day, about what you were grateful for the day before. Of course, they'll be surprised and believe you've gone insane; they'll try to sway you by giving you negative messages.

They may tell a nasty story or just say things like "your attitude is childish, naive, blah blah" in an attempt to pull you down. Don't be influenced by them! Consider who is saying all of this, and recognise that this is most likely not someone you like.

So here's your mission: get rid of the doubters! If your new attitude does not carry them away in a positive way, it signifies you no longer have anything in common with them. These folks will never encourage you, and they may even undermine your decision to be optimistic. You don't need them. Replace a bad habit with a good one—if you want to talk about your life with someone, talk to someone who has the same thinking as you. Tell them how happy you are, what you expect, and how far you've come, and allow them to fill your heart with their happiness.

Look for pleasure within yourself! You will never be truly happy if you constantly expect someone else to entertain you, compliment you, or encourage you to be positive. Expect nothing less than a baseline degree of happiness from anyone. People contribute to your current mindset. They make you happier if you're already happy. If you are upset and they are happy and try to make you happy, you will get even more enraged and resentful. Right? Until you choose to be happy and let happiness overwhelm you.

If you want to do something, now is the time to do it! The moment has come to make a change. Not today, not tomorrow, not next week, not next month... If you want something, don't wait. Do you want to begin a diet? Begin right now. Do you wish to put an end to your smoking habit? Put down the cigarette you're holding. Action is hindered by wasting time. Have you decided to be more self-assured? Begin practising right away!

And here's the key: practice makes perfect. All of the things mentioned require diligent and serious practice. Nobody will be able to pass all of the tests the first time around. You might fail the first time, the second, and even the eighth. Even if you concentrate extremely hard, you may have nasty thinking in the morning, tell yourself again that you can't achieve something, or allow negative feedback to crush you. That's OK. Embrace it and continue to practice. It's a huge accomplishment to fail for the tenth time—it implies you attempted nine more times after the first failure. Please don't give up!! Perhaps this will be the 11th and final time.

It is therefore not good enough to practice a few times; you must be persistent. Repeating the process. There will come a time when you discover that it no longer requires such intense concentration since it has become a habit. You won't be able to recall the last time you weren't able to maintain your cheerful attitude. Smile and the world will reciprocate.

With the 30-day warm-up resilience tasks below, you can begin reconditioning and transitioning your mind and body for positive change today. Over a month, there will be a challenge for each day.

You can become used to dealing with uncertainty by picking a number between 1 and 30 at random every day for a month and looking up the problem it corresponds to on the list below. You can also work your way through the list from 1 to 30. In either case, you'll be faced with fresh daily problems.

The goal of each task is to do it whether you like it or not, whether it seems pointless, dumb, or stupid...Do you have the flexibility to do it? Can you take a risk and try something new? Can you let go of your inhibitions, use humour, and deal with the uncertainty of the task and the outcome?

1. Introduce yourself by saying, "Hello, how are you?" to five random people you don't know with a smile

2. Make a game to challenge your friends to incorporate humorous or odd phrases into everyday conversations. The expressions of Chris Kamara, the famed hilarious British football presenter: "I don't know, Jeff" or "It's unbelievable, Jeff," or something like "razzamatazz," "fandabidozi," "cowabunga," "Willy Wonka"... Basically, having a good time coming up with your unexpected humorous phrases and incorporating them into ordinary discourse. It's innocent fun, and it functions as a small dare, forcing you to step beyond your comfort zone. You'll almost certainly make a few other folks giggle as well.

3. Start a friendly conversation with a stranger or acquaintance, say something entertaining or unusual, in person or over email.

4. Be assertive and truthful; speak out (within reason!) Don't be afraid to say what's on your mind. Things you might not have dared to say otherwise, such as anything you don't particularly like or agree with! Allow yourself to be free for a day - test your limits.

5. Don't be afraid to try anything new.

. . .

6. Wear something brighter, smarter, more glamorous; informal if you're used to feeling "stiff" in your clothing all day – anything that would make you feel better! Change your hair colour or style, your make-up, or do without make-up entirely, grow a beard or moustache, or shave it all together... By now, you've probably figured out what we are talking about. In any event, take note of how different you feel.

7. Make that long-overdue phone call, or call a family member or friend you haven't spoken to in a long time. Listen to your voicemails and make a strategy to face what you've been avoiding.

8. Turn off your phone and social media for a full 24 hours — it's incredibly liberating and surely challenges boundaries!

9. Travel alone – Especially in a new environment.

10. Purchase a copy of The Big Issue (a street newspaper sold by homeless people or those at risk of becoming homeless, allowing them to earn a respectable income) and speak with the seller about how they came to be selling it. And, if you've got it in you, try selling a few to give the seller a break. If you live somewhere where The Big Issue isn't available, do something similar: give a homeless person a drink, take them to lunch, and listen to their tale, or think of another act of kindness you can do — for a stranger in need or perhaps a new coworker.

11. Meditate.

. . .

12. The best way to begin is to gaze into your own eyes and declare to yourself, "I love who I am, and I appreciate what I do." Ask yourself, "Do I have the courage to change my life? Do I respect myself enough to do it?"

13. Use a different form of conveyance. Stop driving your car and use public transportation, walking, or bike instead. You can always learn to drive, whether you'd like to or not. Parking farther away from your location will just increase your travel time.

14. When it gets a bit uncomfortable or difficult, just change things around, even if (especially if!) doing so makes it a little less pleasant or easy.

15. Don't be the same every day. Try something new and enjoy each week to change things up.

16. Reinvent yourself and do something unusual, even if it feels odd at first. It's harmless to you or anyone else. It's great to get to see a place you've never been before. Finding where you are and where you are going may be a great ride. If you don't feel courageous, go to a restaurant or coffee bar you've never been to before. It's also useful to feel where you can go without using your GPS sat nav.

17. Loosen up and let your hair down. Do things like dancing around the house to loud music such as "Who Let The Dogs Out?" Consider performing stand-up comedy, hosting your stand-up comedy show, or going to a comedy event.

. . .

18. Surprise someone with something kind in an unexpected way. Showing your appreciation can either be as simple as complimenting someone or giving someone a price. Alternatively, buying someone flowers or taking them out for lunch without having done anything other than surprising them is a great way to express gratitude.

19. Let the children go play on the adventure playground. For numerous reasons, this is very liberating, exciting, and challenging.

20. For the day, go vegan or abstain from eating sugar, gluten, caffeine, alcohol, and smoking.

21. To CREATE A "LIFE LIST," instead of using the phrase "bucket list," use words like "experience" and "culture."

22. INSTEAD OF SAYING "YES" to something you truly don't want to do, say "no."

23. Pick something entirely different while you're out to eat or at a café.

24. There is a way for you to give up your control. This might be granting your children freedom to decide something you usually handle or granting a coworker control and passing it over to your partner, letting your partner make all of the decisions.

. . .

25. Find something you want to learn about and then embark on a new adventure. These may include participating in a fitness club, joining an interest group or society, or commencing a study course or cookery lessons, all of which would be categorised as personal development workshops.

26. Every week, come up with a personal activity you want to participate in. Doing what you enjoy in your time might be as simple as setting aside a couple of hours to accomplish whatever floats your boat, just as long as it's specific and appealing to you.

27. If you do not get a pay rise, you can request a discount!

28. To enhance yourself or your life, ask others what they enjoy about you and what recommendations they would give you. Use a list of things you appreciate about yourself and the skills you have to understand your positive traits and skills better.

29. New things should be created! To build an entertaining game or to start a new business are two of the options.

30. On a random day off, see what you can get yourself into. Go and do something different. Go to the seashore, see a movie at the cinema, visit an art gallery, and book a hotel for the night. Next, surf the web for reduced activities and choose something else.

. . .

31. It is also possible to reply to the query "How are you doing?" or "How did your day go?" with the response "Fantastic, thank you!" And if they ask you why, tell them that you are positively making an impact on society. Regardless of any struggles you may be experiencing that day, do this — this is the resilience bit!

THE FACT that what you do may look insignificant on the surface is compensated by how important it may seem to you. Your concerns, self-confidence, and phobias will determine the outcome. This list will provide its own set of challenges for you, which will allow you to strengthen your resilience and confidence and trigger a positive level of adrenaline, which will assist in inspiring you to reach even greater levels of success. What's equally important to consider is how participation in the 30-day challenges and stretching your boundaries might influence your life in other ways. For a while, allow yourself to be exposed to new people, try new things, or even behave differently. However, it will generate a new law of attraction for you. This could result in you ending up having closer friendships with someone you previously wouldn't have or encountering different opportunities you previously wouldn't have considered. However, the more you push ahead and venture out into the world, the better your opportunities.

6

Fun Ways To Leave Your Comfort Zone

SOME OF US can jump right in when it comes to overcoming our anxieties, but a warm-up beforehand tends to lead to greater performance and better results. Starting with a well-prepared mind is key in this scenario. Use these techniques when it counts.

These two approaches are simple but highly effective: getting into the right state of mind and learning new breathing patterns will both change your mental state in an instant.

Getting In The Zone

This is a common method employed by top-level athletes and military groups. Simplistic but quite effective. It is crucial to be in the appropriate state of mind, calm, and stress-free when completing your assignment. While practised and used correctly, this state eliminates the brain's capacity to access negative emotions, namely fear.

- Keep your eyes focused directly ahead of you, a bit above eye level.

- Take note of the surroundings; size, shape, colour, and purpose.
- At the same time as still focusing on the place above eye level, broaden your vision to 180 degrees on either side of you.
- Begin with a deep breath (in through the nose, count to five) and end with an equally deep breath (out through the mouth, again counting to five) (count to five). Gently visualise how you feel when your breath flows freely like water and oxygenates your entire body with life-force energy.
- Repeat to yourself, "Invigorated and transformed."
- See yourself as a beam of light, beginning in your lower back and travelling through your body. Once the light has enlightened you, you feel revitalised, calm, and relaxed.

Breathing Techniques

Breathing is, of course, something we do every day; however, on autopilot and without much thought, we are generally breathing without concern. Unless something goes wrong, for example, due to panic attacks, various health conditions, anxiety, anger, or, of course, fear, the way we are breathing does not generally require our attention. However, we may considerably improve our overall health as well as our emotional and physical state by paying attention to our breathing.

The process of respiration occurs in our cells. Oxygen deficiency causes nutritional fuel to be oxidised in the presence of oxygen to yield energy, resulting in imbalanced cellular processes and organ failure. Brain injury or death can result from the lack of oxygen to the brain. When we focus on breathing, we can enhance our vitality, helping us feel peaceful and well-rested.

A good way to cultivate these breathing skills is to engage in frequent practice. While dealing with stressful or panicked situations, these breathing techniques can be done "on the spot" to bring the breathing back to normal. You may experience vertigo when using any of these strategies. In this case, pause and let your breathing settle, then drink a glass of water.

Begin by breathing deeply into your nose, exhaling through your mouth (count to four). It can help to draw a circle or clock in your mind.

USE these techniques for restoring life-giving, stress-reducing energy:

- Breathing in the ocean

Fog a mirror by taking a deep breath through your nose and exhaling through your mouth only slightly open. Like the rolling ocean sound, make the process continuous and rhythmic. Do this exercise for five minutes.

TRY THE FOLLOWING FOR LIFE-GIVING, calming energy:

- Ocean Breath

Constant nostril sniffing utilises your abdomen as a "pump" and uses only your nose to inhale and exhale. Do this exercise for five minutes.

Allow yourself to relax and notice the many feelings you are feeling throughout your body. It is also possible that you may realise that you are feeling more energised and relaxed. In the rare event that you sense tingling feelings over your entire body, you are most likely feeling okay.

Changing How You Think

Think about the things you think about and the way you think about them, and it will have an impact on the things you think about.

Thinking differently is necessary to have a different emotional state, and as a result, it is how we can accomplish entirely new behaviours. There are already several ways to go about this, but the only way to approach it is to think differently.

One of the three strategies for overcoming fear and breaking out of our comfort zone is to face the things that we fear and put ourselves in a situation where we have no other option but to perform. To do this, we must begin with small steps and build up our resolve so that mastering our fears becomes an enjoyable stroll instead of a terrifying race.

Reframing

The term means "to give something a different frame" or "to approach your thinking about something in a different way." In other words, reframing changes how we look at something and see it in a more positive and constructive context. Below is a classic example.

CLEANING UP THE 'WHAT-IF'

Imagine having fear about something, leading to you feeling besieged by tons of other negative thoughts, followed by that sickening feeling of being bogged down by all of the negativity. It has escalated to the point where you cannot accomplish anything and is holding you back from your goals.

This has been a terrible experience. We all have something in common. There is one and only one solution to this problem: getting fully comfortable performing a certain action as "cleaning up the what-ifs". Let's say this:

Confront your "what if" anxieties and record what you would say to yourself if you had such thoughts, for example:

- If I'm not good enough, what will happen?
- What if I don't succeed?
- What if I am made fun of and humiliated, and I regret it?
- What if I cannot afford it?
- What if people assume I'm strange, foolish, or crazy?

Your "what-ifs" don't matter since they're holding you back. Also, remember to record any unpleasant feelings they cause, like embarrassment, humiliation, despair, disappointment, and frustration.

After that, ask yourself:

- "What could go wrong if . . .?"

Did you ever get embarrassed or humiliated in school because you made a mistake? Everything is significant, even if it may not appear that way at first.

At this point, you are probably wondering what it is. Given that, you will conclude that whatever it is, it won't kill you, or it is very unlikely to! Either you're dealing with rational fear, or you're probably experiencing a mix of emotional and rational fear, and you should look into the law of attraction and Quantum reality to try to identify why.

RETURNING to the original point

Take a minute to jot down the logical questions that you can ask about your what-ifs to find out the further implications that they may hold. Then, view the reverse — the opposite which will present itself when you change your thought process, like:

- What if you're just as talented as you think you are, and you're successful beyond your wildest dreams?
- What if you perceive everything as feedback that helps you move forward and try things out?

Don't be embarrassed about having faith in yourself and striving to obtain your goals.

Perhaps you're looking for an investor or the appropriate opportunity but aren't ready to commit yet.

It's a matter of personal projection and limitations; therefore, it's more about the other person than you.

If you're willing to look and believe in what you want, what if many individuals will support and assist you in every way?

For example, when you work on your what-ifs, you will notice that your negative thinking patterns linked with worry gradually release, just as with any attached negative energy to the overwhelming sensation previously stated. Keep in mind that as you advance through the chapters to come, your way of thinking and your underlying belief system will alter, which results in you losing stored negative energy. That said, it is a great feeling to know that your life is about to take a dramatic turn for the better.

Changing a series of 'what-ifs' is possible to shift a scenario, but you can also focus on these to find more solutions. This helps you to move your concentration away from stress and toward planning and problem-solving. In other words:

Don't give up if you're not as skilled as you'd want. Consider what fresh or additional training you need. Where could this lead you?

Could you use the support of others if that isn't suitable for you? It might give you an extra period to devote to something else, which could produce a superior result. Taking a little break may allow you to work more productively.

Instead of thinking no one will aid you financially, think

about replacing "The appropriate person will help" with "the right person will appear." Funding and investment might be a tough endeavour, but don't always imply that no one is interested or unattainable. It tends to be that you are looking for the right individuals or organisations at the wrong time. Deep, often unconscious beliefs such as "I don't deserve it" or "I'm not worthy and capable of earning investment are worth considering."

So, rather than admitting that you cannot obtain investment, try to think about all of the various points you must examine to obtain it.

Your thoughts on embarrassment are subject to shift in context as well. To put it another way, isn't it more shameful to give up on something you've worked hard for, even if you've done everything in your power to get it than to display courage and resolve while going all out in pursuit of it?

HABITUAL THINKING And Changing Those Habits

When a phobia has persisted for a long time, we may have developed a pattern of thinking about it — and as we now know, thinking leads to feelings, and feelings control our behaviour. Finally, when other people are aware of our expressing a particular fear, phobia, or behaviour, we may feel obligated to hold on to that fear, phobia, or behaviour, or we may choose to prolong or enhance a feeling. Nonetheless, even if this is the case, we may instantly transform our mindset if we put in a little effort. Some ways to work on seeing things from a new perspective include:

When you consider what else your fear or constraint might mean, you can identify all the things you've learned from it, the life lessons you've learned, and the resources you will need to obtain to overcome it.

Looking at the several meanings of words that are perceived positively. If you discover yourself employing language that reduces your confidence in your ability to succeed, replace fear-inflicting words with confidence-building ones. The Word Exchange table below is meant to be used as a guide.

Could you rewire your fear to make it a source of empowerment instead? For example, if you were scared of clowns, then it would be a phobia. Being the clown at a charity event will help you deal with this situation. Do you have any fears about yourself? Do you have the ability to make things hilarious and have fun while also helping others?

7

The Art Of Self-Questioning

INTERROGATING yourself can help in all sorts of situations when you're feeling afraid or in unfamiliar territory. It can even resolve the issue by getting to the root of the problem. You use a method of deduction to arrive at this conclusion (gradually breaking things down). So this encourages you to face and test your obstacles because you now know that certain things aren't a problem after all.

QUESTIONS FOR YOURSELF

It's of no relevance now, correct? Do you genuinely feel like it's necessary for the big things of life? Is it worth risking my health for this stress, anxiety, or fear?

If I were to die tomorrow, would there have been any point in being so fearful and wasting time over it?

Would stressing over it at the moment matter or make any difference?

How will fear help you accomplish anything if something is already set in motion? The best, most productive activity is to take whatever action is needed to attain the best potential outcome in a particular situation.

Am I working in the right direction? My main goal is to

discover what my main purpose and intention is — the big picture. Is my state of stress and worry enabling me to maintain a proper focus? Be mindful of the corner apartment and focus on what you see. Even if you are aware of other things, you see just what you focus on.

How does something exactly go wrong? What are the impeding factors keeping me from finding a solution and progressing?

Is there anything I could have done to be more resourceful? How can I handle this? Which resources am I able to utilise? Is there anything I can be thankful for and express thanks for?

If fear is indeed a waste of life, then what good is it? What does it have that I like so much? Could this be anything to like? Is there an alternate, more productive, and healthier way to enjoy this?

8

Change Your Focus

INSTEAD OF TELLING your mind to spew profanities with "I can't do it!"

Instead, have fun repeating something nice or something ridiculous.

Make an effort and enjoy yourself." If you're going to do it, go ahead and do it now. .! Ding".

"Screw it, just do it." (often used previously, but excellent advice nonetheless.) — Richard Branson, an entrepreneur from the UK.

Jeff: "Unbelievable, Chris" — British sports commentator Chris Kamara.

Use several voices and dialects to be innovative. Instead of using your favourite quotes, use renowned ones you stumble across.

Create An Outcome

For example, if you cannot have something (a certain something) unless you perform "x," then "x" is the prize you receive.

Take responsibility for your actions.

Instead of telling someone your plans, which makes it

more difficult to get out of doing what you have planned, tell them what you're planning to do to be more motivated to go through with it. There are various possible motivations for doing anything creative. For example, you might do something creative for charity, your boss, or your friends; alternatively, you might publicly express something through social media.

This is a fantastic approach because it puts you in the space, making it difficult to turn back on your promise and afford you few alternatives other than simply carrying out your word.

Model Someone And Pretend

We become what we pretend and practice! Before acting, pretend to be someone who you want to be more confident, bold, or humorous. Also, adopt their good characteristics, such as their appearance and manner of speaking, personal ideals, and approach to everything, as if you were performing an impersonation of them.

If you find it difficult to project someone's appearance, do your best to mimic them, whether you know someone, a television character, or even a movie character. Even if you're only creating a passing impression, making those adjustments requires making modifications in your brain to influence your physical self to achieve the impression. Doing this will major impact your feelings and behaviours or perhaps help you do something you want.

Change Your Environment

The shift in your environment can greatly influence your thoughts in two distinct ways:

When you focus on using all your senses to imagine and think you are somewhere else - a secure, pleasant, and joyful location – you provide yourself with that mental respite that relieves stress. You'll sense a surge of positivity as soon as you turn this on, and that will transform your thinking and thus how you feel and consequently how you act.

Remember to provide a pleasant and encouraging environment for those who work with you since negativity begets fear. You will only feel worse when among other individuals who share your worries, phobias, or lack of confidence. However, if you're around by positive, proactive people, it will help you realise that you need to take control of your life and focus on positivity to turn your situation around. Conventional thinking can be used to explain this because two agoraphobics sharing an apartment would likely not leave the building very often. The chances are that if an agoraphobic individual lived with a good and encouraging person, this person would help their companion get out and about more.

Visualisation

Great achievements can be achieved through visualisation if it is correctly understood and utilised. Our minds naturally think in pictures, and engaging all our senses to do so also helps us form memories, resulting in changes in our physical state.

With the use of PET scan technology, we know that, regardless of whether subjects are vividly imagining something or experiencing it in reality, the same regions of the brain are activated; this toxin and nerve-activation are identical to the point that the mind can influence the body in the same way.

For the sake of argument, pretend that the autopilot in our brain that is responsible for running and sustaining our bodies 24/7 cannot tell the difference between truth and illusion.

This occurs when you have a vivid, realistic dream and wake up crying, laughing, or being disturbed. Although it was merely a dream, your body responded as if it were real; thus, it provoked a physical response. If you've experienced a dream like this, you may have had to doubt whether or not the incident occurred.

When it comes to pushing our comfort zones, visualising is quite powerful. The healing process can be aided by visualisation and inducing minor physical changes, such as increasing the temperature. To understand something, we must be able to see, hear, touch, and experience it as vividly as possible.

Dr O. Carl Simonton of the University of Texas found a specific case, published in 1971, in which a 61-year-old man had been diagnosed with throat cancer. His disease was in a very advanced stage; his voice had grown faint, and his weight had plummeted to 98 pounds. Doctors only predicted that he would not respond well to treatment because he was already quite frail, and his prognosis was very poor: doctors assigned him just a 5% chance of survival following treatment. They anticipated that he would not live beyond the time frame given.

He wondered if he could use visualisation to discover a psychological approach. He advised the patient to imagine his immune system targeting and eliminating the cancer cells, followed by their being swept away from his body and replaced with healthy cells. Next, the patient returned and began implementing this visualisation several times each day. The patient's response to radiation was nearly pain-free once the tumour shrank. It faded totally after two months.

In this scenario, mind power was the key factor in the recovery since a positive mindset and belief system encouraged success. During the six-year follow-up period, this same patient went on to employ visualisation to help him combat his arthritis and remain free of both the ailment and cancer, after which he resumed a healthy life. It's a shame that his fear of exploring new ideas hindered his healing.

Concentrate on your anxiety, then imagine yourself floating into the future shortly before the occurrence that is worrying you. See something significant, like a great accomplishment, demonstrating that you've done well and reached your goals.

Don't just wing it; ensure you get into it. When trying to

experience anything from your perspective, view what you can see through your own eyes as if you were experiencing it right now. Perceive the subtleties in what you can perceive. What is being said about it? Are you trying to tell yourself or others something? Finally, experience every pleasant emotion you can - whether warm and comforting or new and exciting experiences. Don't leave out any of your senses; in particular, use all your tastes and scents, if any are present. Don't hold back! Go all out, and you will succeed.

Now commit this to memory. Make sure to lock it down so it doesn't move at all. Immerse the lock in an unyielding substance, then cover it, and leave it alone!

Return to the present, and hold onto that upcoming successful conclusion. Also, if you obsess on something, you will get more of it, so strive to keep it positive. Constantly remind yourself of your desired objective, and work hard to accomplish it. While you are envisioning something, you will also have to take action to make it happen.

Ultimately, in a nutshell, we need to have a very clear idea of what success after the event will look and feel like, and we also need to complete the specific tasks required to help make that vision a reality. If you follow this advice, you will successfully energise anxiety, enabling you to accomplish your goals.

When you boil it all down, most of us have a clear concept of what we want in life, whether we're conscious of it or not. It isn't easy to maintain this balance, though, when we are not always aware of it or lose sight of it for some other reason.

When people begin to lose themselves, experience breakdowns, have midlife crises and get into depression, this is generally when people's expectations and core blueprints no longer align. This sets the stage for additional stress and distraction, which only worsens their emotions of being unfocused, uninitialised, or just spaced out by life. As a result, goals, desires, and ambitions can – and indeed do – fall victim to this type of suffering.

One of the keys to managing the entirety of this is to

know exactly what we want, knowing who we are, who we want to be, and if we're on the right track. Do we allow our ideas of what we "should" be to overtake us, or do we desire to reach these goals? To change our preconceived thoughts and objectives, we must break out of the mould to improve ourselves.

Regardless of your precise ultimate aim, purpose, and intention, whether it is big or tiny, the most important thing is what you are after. The overall goal is to equip people who desire to move outside their comfort zones with the resources they need to accomplish anything they choose. This means that if we're well aware of ourselves and our fears and limits have been erased, anything is possible!

One of the biggest things holding people back from taking the steps necessary to obtain their goals is the fear of the unknown.

9

Getting What You Want

YOU'LL HAVE to admit that if you think about it, those who have firm and unwavering visions about what they want always attain their desires sooner or later, in one way or another. This may often be seen in people because they are driven by an exceptionally intense desire to achieve their goals, and everything they do is channelled in that direction.

Warren Buffett is a wonderful illustration of this. With a net worth of $87.5 billion, Warren serves as the chairman and CEO of Berkshire Hathaway.

We learn a lot from this about our core desires and motivations and how that knowledge shapes our results in life. Our desire for something must be really strong for us to go out and obtain it. It is also important to develop self-awareness to differentiate between what makes the difference and everything else.

Here are a few thought-provoking questions for your consideration:

1. What is your life's mission statement?

. . .

2. Is this *your* plan, or has someone else developed it for you?

3. Are you having fun with this?

4. Is it everything you're doing?

5. As you grow and mature, have your plans and expectations changed?

6. Do you see things differently now?

7. If you are honest enough to confess that you've acknowledged it, have you acted on it?

8. If money was no object, what would you do?

THE QUESTION IS, "What is truly stopping you from pursuing your goals?" It appears that beneath the surface reasoning, a hidden layer is at work. This layer gives you the true solution.

For you to meet your goals, what must transpire? And what else do you want? And what else did you discover? And be on the lookout for new issues for as long as necessary, asking "what else and how" until you finally reach your answers.

Are you now confident and willing to put everything on the line to win? All your talents, thoughts, and imagination will be completely utilised? That is what sets it apart.

. . .

Behaviour

- Is there something you do every day in your effort to realise your dreams?
- Are you maximising all feasible opportunities?
- Are you currently making any alterations?
- Do you positively discuss this frequently?
- How do you write?
- Do you intend to "attempt" to do something, "wishing" it might work out? OR is something genuinely happening right now?

If you truly believe in what you're doing, you must know the language of the latter.

Another interpretation is that you are not given the time to think about it. You do not have the time for it. Instead, you expect it to happen, similar to having a fantastic website and expecting a large number of people.

The most important step is to make sure your behaviour matches your actual goals. When you don't see an opportunity to help, ask yourself if you want this.

You will only have success if you truly want it and act as if you will attain it by doing everything necessary for it to come true.

Instead of having dreams, strive towards expectations.

Personality

You are who you are, and you want to grow into someone better.

- What are the attributes you need to show to accomplish your goals?
- Is this an appropriate way to express your current personality?

If an impartial buddy can provide good external feedback, this could be valuable!

By being more aware of your true motivations, you will discover exactly why you may encounter difficulties on your path to your goals, even though you are doing everything perfectly and feel that everything is aligned.

ENVIRONMENT

- Do you spend time with people who are similar to you and put yourself in locations where you're likely to meet people who are similar to you?
- Do you rely on those around you to help you reach your goal? Or when you're in a dull environment, do you lose your motivation, get discouraged, and feel your spirits go down?
- Do you ever meet people that seem to have nothing to do with your projects yet end up unexpectedly helping you with what you're working toward? If nothing has changed, then what is stopping you from asking those questions?
- Are they the right people/individuals to assist you in moving forward? Do they move in step, or do they get in the way?
- Why aren't they aligned and devoted enough to overcome these obstacles?
- What are you going to do to give yourself the best chance of succeeding?

The importance of this last aspect cannot be overstated; as aforementioned, negativity tends to spark like wildfire and hence impairs progress and motivation. An analogy is like a bucket of crabs: the crabs on top are mostly just crawling on top of one another, but one crab is struggling to break free and is slowly making its way up the bucket, eventually making it to the top. On the other hand, all the other crabs are constantly pulling it back down, thus slowing the "freedom crab's" progress and mission.

Try to imagine what would happen if all the other crabs were to cooperate and help push it higher.

Practicalities

- Does your skillset, knowledge base, and aptitudes support your goals?
- Do you think they are up to the task of enabling you to be more social? Or Could this be an unconscious issue that is keeping you from progressing?
- Is it realistic to accomplish your goals if they don't match these criteria?

Without this key ingredient, it isn't easy to move on because we must build our talents and resources before proceeding. Change tends to happen in a significant way when we are prepared and equipped.

Beliefs and Values

As you have already learned and will undoubtedly have engraved in your brain after reading this book, the most crucial part of everything you want to accomplish is your beliefs and values. You won't have the actual drive and ambition to achieve what you want until you have your basic beliefs, and that is something you want to stick to.

It is necessary to have a clear-cut goal to propel you forward. Your blueprint is encoded into your DNA and the entirety of your brain — and this is not simply a metaphor!

Once you've finished this book, you'll know whether you're 100% behind your final goal or whether you may need to adjust your plan.

10

Making Your Life GREAT

THIS BOOK COVERS all the aspects covered in GREAT and then explains how to implement them completely.

G - GOALS & Outcome

Design a comprehensive aim that is distinct and specific to your audience.

Without a goal and an outcome, we are merely wandering and existing. So we won't be able to take advantage of life and fail to enjoy it, which means we may miss out on some of life's best moments.

We know that, in keeping with Locke and Latham's classic goal theory, creating goals increases performance. Furthermore, having a particular aim rather than a general or unclear one greatly impacts reaching the objective.

Every successful outcome begins with a goal, but it is important to identify, measure, and align these objectives with a compelling reason, focus, and motive to turn these objectives into concrete outcomes. If you have the time, you should investigate these suggestions in greater detail.

. . .

R - Responsibility

Personal responsibility NOT reasons.

Ultimately, in every context, consistent with all outstanding mindsets, comes a deep-seated feeling of personal responsibility – "What can I do to make a difference?"

The fact that you must accept responsibility for helping yourself is conveyed here. Always focus on finding new ways to help the issue; and finding out what and how you need to change, rather than placing the blame elsewhere or expecting someone else to help.

This is about self-mastery because while everything else may be out of your control, you can always shape your thoughts and perceptions. Seeing the benefits rather than letting the bad leap out is associated with it.

When you decide to take control of your life and change things for the better, you are not a victim or a martyr.

This process moves the transformation forward and provides greater desirable effects on multiple levels.

E - Emotional Well-being and Ever-Positive, Humorous Mindset

Without an emotional and positive state of mind, the rest is unlikely to manifest in its best form.

The lack of positive emotions significantly impacts the restrictions, blockages, and illnesses that we all experience. Also, for success in any situation, it is important to have the ability to both constructively and proactively deal with emotional issues for enhanced well-being.

Attributable to this, it is imperative to have a good outlook, to never lose sight of:

Here is a summary of what you can do: you are a problem-solver and have a sense of humour on your journey to success.

To have a positive mindset, you should be grateful for all the resources and talents you have. You should also appreciate all your experiences for providing you with great learning opportunities. If you're using one, use your gratitude rock here. Touch it whenever you're glad and appreciative, and this will make you more appreciative and grateful, helping you to get even more of what you want.

Always remember to appreciate the struggles and the wonderful opportunities that result from them. Even when you have strong feelings, there is always something nice to discover.

A - Awareness and Absence of Panic

When your course of action appears to be veering off course, strive to enhance your knowledge of yourself and stay calm.

Whatever success you achieve will be accompanied by increased self-awareness, enabling you to recognise when you're running low on energy and the following changes you may need to make. You'll have a stronger understanding of your intuition so you can discover how you need to develop and further utilise it for higher success effectively.

Panic and the emotions that go with it are vital to prevent when things don't go according to plan. Trust in yourself and the process. That is how strong your belief is. When you know your blueprint, you can trust yourself and the process to keep going when you face those obstacles.

T - Total Unshakable Belief System

If someone has made it to the top and accomplished their goals, they will always have had absolute faith in their mission and their goals.

This must be in your DNA. If you have this, you will face challenges head-on, regardless of the reason, and prevail.

So if you have any questions, get to the root of the problem and figure out the why.

Are you convinced that you're going to succeed?

Is this really what you want?

Are you simply experiencing a restriction of energy that you need to eliminate?

This is of essential importance because you get the impression of what you truly believe at the subliminal level. Remember, this is the factor that will allow you to obtain whatever you desire. If you are certain of your beliefs and have no reservations, you will complete your mission and become your goals.

Use GREAT as an efficient yet powerful reminder to remain that way in any context you choose.

11

Other Elements In Determining Drive And Direction

SUCCESSFUL RESULTS ARE possible on either end of the spectrum when goals and objectives are concerned.

It's common for people to be so dedicated and focused on the goals that they end up worrying about it and creating unnecessary stress for themselves. They pose the question, "Why haven't we done it yet?" and assume, "I must be doing everything wrong."

This is the sum of all this, which leads to feelings of irritation, annoyance, demotivation, weariness, and so on. Furthermore, note where statements like this are directing your attention — they're not about what you desire!

In the opposite case, forcing a solution and a goal results in being unable to come up with anything since creativity is stifled. All of this produces feelings of anxiousness and absolute confusion, leading to sentiments of hopelessness and despair as a result.

Other than those already stated, the key reasons for this are as follows: To enable natural time, and for both young and old people to trust the process of life because the above two conditions indicate they have not fully developed that unwavering belief system and are not completely in agreement with their core plans and blueprint. Quite simply, the time will arrive when you are "truly" ready.

Results are important, but getting everything else in the place is just as necessary. Let things be; put everything to the test and see what happens. Concentrate on your positive core beliefs and general thinking to bring positivity back into your life without opposition.

When all the required factors are in place and you take the time to breathe, your wishes will come true.

"The pitcher needs a still cup for divine alchemy to work."

Thus, once all of the necessary components are in place, believe in nature to act naturally. It takes hard work, determination, and a strong head to accomplish something, but you can achieve it if you have everything in place.

So if you believe otherwise, really get to work on figuring out why. Start by thinking about yourself and personal responsibility, then build on that by working on your emotional well-being and happiness. When you are ready to discover the answers, they will be there.

Regardless of whether we decide to take major steps toward change or take modest measures up to that transformation, we still need to be motivated to go forward.

Although we may frequently believe we are not ready to face anything, the issue is a matter of motivation.

As mentioned before, to succeed in life, we must have a strong and well-defined motivation to succeed. It has to be critical enough for us to motivate us to take action, or we'll fail to devote enough attention or energy to deal with it.

It may be necessary to be upset about something to do something. A rather uncommon but severe scenario is when people have to go through a health crisis or personal emergency before changing their habits.

Alternatively, we may have already reached our intended state, for example, by setting a goal to shed pounds to improve our health, look slimmer for a wedding or a picture shoot, or participate in a marathon or other charity athletic event.

The bottom line is: We must be motivated enough to act when something affects us and remain committed and enthusiastic in pursuing our goal.

When you are presented with the following question, ask yourself, "How motivated do I feel about this?" Then, immediately jot down your answers as they first occur to you in list form.

What's most important to you about living?

When you make a list, issues that are first on your mind and which you place at the top will be essential. While creativity occurs in the unconscious mind, it comes from the goal-getter – your unconscious mind – rather than the goal-setter – your conscious mind – which happens when you've had time to analyse, discuss, and make a list of what you think the importance of the order should be. Your values will also be reflected in the order of the list, which is critical since they help you to set your goals and determine your motivation to act.

So did the highest intention of your goal – happiness, freedom, fulfilment (or your representation of these) – come near or at the top of your list?

Is your goal critical enough to you right now to sustain you and keep you committed to action?

If you wanted a bit more motivation, consider your higher purpose and why you're doing what you're doing. What do we need to address? What are you unwilling to do? Continue, and you will succeed!

If you are still having trouble in your drive and value area, consider consulting with a master practitioner of NLP or professional hypnotherapy.

Doing everything in this book will likely yield remarkable results if you're focused on obtaining happiness, freedom, fulfilment, or whatever results from releasing your fear. Go for it and stay focused! You may encounter new worries as you go through this process; the ability to fight your concerns and take steps that push you out of your comfort zone will allow you to reach your goals. Although this event can occur when you are least expecting it, don't be deterred. Take the time to savour and appreciate the process during the journey.

Positive Supports to Keep Driving Your Direction

Deciding to venture outside of our comfort zone and breaking down barriers are two very important decisions that we must make. This is because we hesitate before making decisions or procrastinate over the outcomes, which means we don't move forward into new terrain. In other words, but as soon as we can trust our ability to make decisions, we open up new avenues for pushing our boundaries because there's always a reaction directing us toward that goal.

Deciding between two or more possible choices is something we do every day. However, we all know that simplicity doesn't always mean an easy thing.

The problems arise when we focus on making the "best" selection and get concerned with the different ramifications of our choice; there might not always be a "best" option among the options available. So, we must do our best with the resources and knowledge we have and go with it, even if the outcome is either good, wrong, or irrelevant at the time; it will ultimately be in the best interest of the long-term viability of our business.

No matter what route you take, you will, in the end, attain your goal that truly suits your pattern. Making a "wrong" decision at the time just means you have the opportunity to guide the path in whatever ways you may. If you make decisions out of unconscious learnings or motivations, you are, of course, the one who dictates the path. To say something is an intermediate step is not to say it's necessarily "bad." It merely means it's another step in the process of learning, obtaining resources, appreciating, and moving on.

We can work with our decisions and choices when possible, but at the moment when it's difficult, we must leave our comfort zone and think critically:

- What does life teach us?
- We should learn something from this event; what should it be?
- Where are we going from here?
- In this task, has it brought us into contact with someone we wouldn't have otherwise? What are such persons or things useful for?
- What was it like for you?
- Have you gained the ability to talk about your story because of it? Is writing a book in your blood?

Although there are many questions like this, the answers will be diverse and unique to everyone, but they always hold the potential to shine a light on your unconscious thoughts and progress along your journey. For instance, do you draw in difficult situations and make incorrect decisions due to your unconscious sense of punishment? When you think about it, do you perhaps believe that you're getting what you were always destined to have only after you've gone through a period of difficulty or events that you believed you had to endure to earn it?

It would be best to examine this idea more closely to discover that no decision is ever bad for you. It just aligns with your desire to construct your world and meet your requirements.

Despite this, we may lessen the stress of our progress by making good selections to assist us along the way.

Even if your decisions prevent you from correcting past mistakes, you should embrace all the learning as it helps you to make better decisions in the future.

Intuition and rationality can both be used to make decisions, but a strong blend of the two results in the best decision.

EFFECTIVE STEPS in fearless decision-making

Reduce the number of complex decisions and turn each into a simpler step. You might approach this by inquiring about the overall objective of the decision and what your goal is in deciding on it. The overall goal of performing what you do is to further your cause. It corresponds with your decision.

List every solution or possibility and go over it with reliable, well-balanced, and unbiased people. Making things look less complicated and overwhelming is a good way to get started.

Give yourself a time period and a deadline by which you will make decisions.

Necessary information must be obtained.

Weigh the possible risks against the gains by analysing all the possible outcomes.

First, figure out what's most essential to you when making a decision. Is your decision aligned with these priorities?

Which action will result in the best for the greater goal?

You should also consider intuition and facts and logic, as you always should not ignore your gut feeling.

When it comes to making decisions, do you believe you're doing your best, even if the result is negative? When you have clearly expressed your commitment, you have made the ideal decision. Deciding on a course of action is easy yet powerful; a small difference can lead to a big answer.

PRACTICAL SOLUTIONS

When we examine the outcomes of successful people, we may easily assume that they were "lucky". Although this is true, it is also rare that we notice the years of pain, blood, sweat, and tears required to achieve their accomplishment.

Only time, personal experiences, and their unwavering

belief and perspective separate you from people like them.

Listing issues can help us get our mind and belief in the right place, as it allows us to view the problem from multiple angles and discover what measures we need to take to solve it. Additional mental space is also created.

Break three columns on a piece of paper into three columns, each of which is labelled "Problems," "Solution Options," and "Actions."

Create a list of everything that stands in the way of you being successful.

Write below "Resolution & Overcome" every potential solution.

Indicate all the actions you've decided on and give it a checkmark when you've finished them.

It is not ideal or necessarily straightforward, but these unconventional methods are a helpful step in the right direction to eliminate limits that are impeding progress. After this, you'll have the mental room and time needed to concentrate on and release the root issues.

Your "solution action list" is laid out here. It is best to attack the problem piece by bit to avoid any overburden. For the time being, do what you can, when you can. Everything is a positive step in the right direction, and you'll be happy about that in the long run. When you've gone through a difficulty once, tick it off.

If you can perform a small activity every day, you will move closer to a solution, which will also help you keep your focus. Reward yourself as well. This encourages you to keep working and stay motivated.

When you believe wholeheartedly in your cause and sincerely want something, you will discover a way to overcome the hurdles that may come your way. Instead of concentrating on what's wrong, concentrate on finding a solution instead.

Ask yourself as soon as you wake up:

What steps will I take today to make my goal even closer to me?"

12

Goals With Purpose

As part of **GREAT**, we examined the essential concept of setting attainable goals that will direct the endeavour's success. Here are some easy suggestions that you can use to build a clear aim with a reasonable expectation.

What are your goals and objectives? Do you feel ready to carry out your part of the bargain now?

Every small step you take will help you move toward your objective. Bring this forward by creating an external check: make someone ask you each day about your progress, pledge to send yourself a night email detailing your activities, anything to help you remain accountable and motivated.

To make your goal more precise, measurable, feasible, meaningful, and time-bound, follow these steps:

- Use checkpoints to chart your progress, and reward yourself for each accomplishment.
- Imagine yourself in your ideal future and use all your senses to create a detailed picture of what you imagine.

If you know about SMART goals, you're familiar with this

concept. The outcome must be made crystal clear for goals to become a reality.

To illustrate the distinction between "goals that remain goals" and "goals that you actualise and which have a significant outcome," imagine that you apply the SMART (**S**pecific, **M**easurable, **A**chievable, **R**ealistic, **T**imely) approach alongside GREAT. This procedure, therefore, will assist you in choosing a path.

1. Shape the specifics.

When you know exactly what you're trying to do and how you plan to get there, you get several advantages. Instead, it is better to come up with specific words, like "I want to enhance my health" or "I intend to be successful." Consider clearly what you will improve. When will you reach your goal? In what way? What do you want to achieve? What will you need it for? What are you trying to achieve?

2. Make it measurable.

To know when you've reached your goal, what indicator will you use?

For you to know you've accomplished this, what must happen?

Do you have any evidence?

When can you gauge your success?

If others were unable to tell the difference, how would that person know?

Exactly what does it mean to have gotten what you wanted?

3. Imagine your goal AS IF it is true right now.

The sooner you get a feel for it, the better. Programme it

into your memory so you know what your result will be. Do this using all your senses.

When you have already achieved your aim, look for something new to view.

Understand what you can understand. There you go!" I've accomplished it! Has someone else just congratulated you, or have you just been congratulated?

Now allow yourself to experience the emotions you felt when you reached your goal. Do you have a pleasant, joyful, thrilled, pleased, astonished expression on your face?

Do you notice anything specific? Are you in a specific place?

Is there a distinctive taste? To celebrate your achievement, are you having a drink or anything to eat?

Ensure that you employ all your senses and are as descriptive as possible. You already know how visualisation works via scientific principles, so leverage the great neurology we all have to achieve success!

4. Check to see if your steps are practical, realistic, relevant, and reasonable.

Ideally, you should have multiple choices if the situation calls for it.

Do you have the necessary resources and assistance to accomplish your goal?

Did you allow for a reasonable period to reach this goal?

Are you in the appropriate frame of mind and committed to achieving your goals?

Are you fully committed to it?

Is this really what you want?

Are you ready to try something else to help you attain your goal?

Other resources and information are available to you; what else do you need?

In case obstacles arise, what else can you do to help yourself?

5. Give yourself adequate time, and don't leave the decision open-ended.

In closing, remember to be realistic, but be as explicit as possible. Your unconscious mind will answer in no time with the month, date, and year you will have accomplished your goal.

This will help you get an accurate picture of your results and provide your mind with a focused target. Conjure up the situation as if it's already a reality. Don't forget to leave your ideas in your mind.

Don't be hesitant to set a date with your crush. Don't expect it to happen when you anticipate it, and don't expect it to happen the way you envisioned (consciously at least).

When you implement all the SMART steps diligently, you will embed them into your physiology, causing you to become focused and, in turn, resulting in increased energy and results. Also, bear in mind how our thoughts work and imagine your goal. Knowing our outcome can be favourably programmed and preset into our entire neurology to obtain the precise results we want.

13

Getting Outside Your Comfort Zone Under Any Circumstances

How can I get outside my comfort zone at work?

IF YOU STICK to your norm, you'll be stagnant and miss out on various challenges and opportunities to grow. Findings indicate that productivity, creativity, and the ability to cope with change can be considerably increased by moving beyond one's comfort zone and engaging in activities that cause healthy anxiety levels. Here are some tips to help you break free from your workplace comfort zone.

1. Ask for something new

Changing your assigned work is one of the fastest methods to make your life a lot more interesting. The ultimate goal is not to increase the amount of work you're already carrying in your calendar, but to provide an opportunity for a new type of challenge to trigger you to think and behave differently than previously. You're not only helping the firm and your coworkers by taking on a new project or joining a new initiative, but you're helping yourself as well. Not many businesses have a shortage of work, so if you're the first to raise your hand to work on a new project or deliverable, you can almost guarantee that it will be yours. Being asked to do more tasks will not only necessitate new approaches to productivity, but it will also present new opportunities to interact with people, processes, or technology you haven't before.

2. Address your fears

Occasionally, people stay in their safe haven because it shields them from activities they're afraid of or dislike. Whether you're afraid of talking in public or flying in planes, it may be time to tackle those fears. It may be advantageous to attend a public speaking course if you have trouble speaking in front of a group of people. The more charts and graphs in a report, the more whirling it will make your head spin. If this is the case, locate an online course on quantitative analysis or enlist the support of a colleague to figure out how to analyse the current corporate sales report. It will be that much easier to conquer phobias if you've taken the first steps.

3. Learn new technology

Every area of professional life is now affected by technology. The evolution and change in the way people work that continues to be wrought by video, chat, and collaboration platforms are moving faster than ever. You can escape your comfort zone by using new technology that enhances your productivity, offers you additional communication options, and empowers you to work alongside your colleagues. Another useful example is an app that connects to your work calendar and keeps you from scheduling yourself too far ahead. Alternatively, knowing how to program simple macros in Excel could boost your analytical skill. Whether you're an entry-level employee or a C-suite executive, various technology-based solutions can assist you in doing your work more efficiently and productively.

. . .

4. Get a new job

Perhaps the ultimate way to leave your work comfort zone is by moving into a new job. People may see this as an apparent decision, however shifting to a new industry or industry can be an immense challenge. One of the primary reasons why many people stay in their jobs for longer than they should is because they are fearful of losing their job stability and being fearful of being left behind in their job and the transition to the unknown. The majority of people will quit their employment sometime throughout their working years. The most recent BLS tenure survey found that, on average, employees stay with their current employers for 4.2 years before looking for new work. Finding a new job may be precisely what you need to jump-start your career and take on a new endeavour.

WHEN YOU VENTURE into new and unfamiliar terrain, it might be challenging. Regardless, dealing with situations that shake your personal beliefs and working approach will assist you in succeeding through times of uncertainty. You can always escape your comfort zone and reinvigorate your career no matter what path you take.

14

How Can I Get Outside My Comfort Zone In My Relationships?

ONCE YOU HAVE SPENT a significant amount of time with your partner, you have undoubtedly gotten into a comfortable rhythm together. It is not uncommon, and on certain occasions, it might be pleasant to curl up on the couch for the weekend. However, when you have no such trips with your significant other, you will both be left unfulfilled. It is easy to get comfortable and stick to the same daily routine if you believe that your 'comfort zone is the only place you spend your time.

The method you use to get out of your comfort zone in your relationship is important since it should be scheduled in the calendar and linked to something they anticipate or look forward to. Here are some suggestions to help you try something new: novelty is essential.

TAKE a mini holiday

If you want to take your relationship to a new level, you should go on an excursion without your significant other. "When we travel to new locations, we find new parts of ourselves together." "We're jolted out of our daily routine, which allows us to be more receptive to trying new things. We also feel more liberated when we don't have what we usually have. This is good for the relationship because it may be relaxing and freeing. It can revitalise it completely."

SCHEDULE A WEEKLY DATE night

Is it safe to say that you've never been on a real date? Do you like to go to fancy restaurants, where you make a reservation, dress up, and stay the night talking about anything and everything? Romance should be added to your calendar if it's been a while. "Studies show that having a date night once a week considerably helps marriages and those who are cohabiting. It boosts sexual satisfaction, reduces the divorce rate, and adds romance, "Sherman comments. They have time to focus on one another and are the greatest version of themselves because of it.

CAMP OUTSIDE and change your routine

Although having the opportunity to slip into your cosy bed every night is great, changing up your nightly routine from time to time will lead to some exciting recollections. If you want to step out of your comfort zone, being innovative may be quite useful. "Go someplace where you've never been or eaten before. It is possible to get your love life and sex life back on track just by travelling or sleeping under the moonlight. It indicates that you care and are putting effort into your relationship by going the additional mile to mix things up."

Do something risky together

Doing so doesn't imply you have to jump off of a plane. At any rate, why not? The faster your team's adrenaline is stimulated, the stronger your relationship becomes. Sherman advises passengers to go on a hot air balloon flight, trek in the mountains, or zip-lining. "Research has shown that trying new and challenging activities will raise one's interest. Plus, it's exhilarating to lead a far more exciting life than the one you've been leading so far. When you take a risk, you will strengthen your relationships and make clear memories."

ENROL IN A CLASS

You do not have to quit learning just because you have left school. Preparing to enrol in a class you and your spouse have never done before could be difficult, but it will open up long-term development capabilities. "If you have a class with a dress code, consider going to a ballroom dance class, a cooking class, or even an art class. When you learn something new, you get into a development mindset, which frees you from your previous level of comfort, "Sherman comments. By participating in this activity, you'll begin to have a similar interest and spur some exploration in your relationship.

RECREATE the beginning

Even if your relationship seems boring and lazy, think back to when it was passionate and vibrant. Think back to your first date. It may be cheesy to try to recreate this moment, so simply remember the first few months of your relationship. Saying things like those first impressions, those embarrassing moments, and the early days of a relationship helps to bring some of that first love back.

AMP up the sex

Often, if the relationship is going nowhere, the sex is as well. Getting things moving again can be accomplished through anything from a new job position to moving to a new place or simply having a little sexual fun. Once you have renewed that connection, it will likely affect other aspects of your relationship.

SAY what you appreciate about each other

You need reminders of why you love each other every once in a while. Your partner needs to hear it, as well as you saying it. For example, reminding yourself how vital you are to each other can help break you out of a loop. In no case does anyone want to be taken for granted, and reconnecting and renewing your relationship will benefit you.

LEARN new things about each other

Remember how you used to play Twenty Questions with your crush in elementary school? Of course, you may have asked questions on broad topics, such as "What do you like to eat?" when you initially started dating, you'd say, "What's #1 on your bucket list?" to get to know each other, but as time went on, you should keep asking questions to get to know one other better. According to Sherman, "Get a book of questions and discover things about your spouse that you've never known." "You may think you know everything about your spouse after being together for a long time, but you should still keep asking questions to avoid the stagnation that occurs when you think you know everything about your spouse. The search is never-ending. Doing this exercise opens yourself up to your relationship in new ways, and your partner is doing the same for you. So, it will help you remember to make an effort to speak with your friends and family daily."

BE MORE vulnerable

Quite alarming. Even if you've been together for a long time, it isn't easy to let your defences down completely. People want to reveal who they are, but exposing yourself will build a profound and irreplaceable bond. Sherman describes his feelings of being real and vulnerable as "forcefully" taking him out of his comfort zone. "Talk about your concerns and experiences and things that make you feel vulnerable. This will strengthen your relationship, entwining you with your partner and building trust."

15

Fail Hard But Learn Fast

THERE's a common expression in the sports world that "Winning hides all."

To understand the idea behind the saying, just think about it this way. The major purpose of a sports team is to win; thus, when they win, they don't need to work on their shortcomings or defects because the flaws have not affected their success. They won the game. When a sports team wins 20 games in a row, they adopt a negative attitude known as "Who cares, we'll win regardless" that does more harm than good to their growth and learning.

Losing, in this instance, is beneficial since it enables us to learn more about ourselves. Sometimes failure is the best way to reveal a weakness or a blind spot. After a loss, athletes identify techniques or approaches that didn't work and learn from their mistakes. Improvement and growth are parents to each other. Failure is dealing with obstacle after obstacle to overcome them.

In failure, you will learn and grow the most. Confront failure head-on and learn from it. Even if you decide you want to fail, don't be concerned about it. This is saying that, no matter how hard you try, it is still possible to fall short of the mark.

That being said, first of all, it is inevitable. What happens is that we aren't always able to attract every person we desire, we're unable to secure every job we apply for, and our cooking techniques aren't flawless every time. No one can escape failure, and it offers us the opportunity to grow. If you are unsuccessful at something, you have the ability to gain valuable information, like how to attract people better, what will make a better impression during a job interview, and how much salt you should use in jambalaya. When you succeed every time, you don't go through the process of course correction.

Failure is inevitable, so be prepared for it and respond differently. When you identify possible issues, you are forced to scrutinise your strategy and look for ways to improve your approach. One can have complete faith in something; nonetheless, it is still essential to have life preservers and inflatable rafts on board, even if the shipbuilder himself has complete faith in his ships.

The ability to look critically at your shortcomings and other people's is one of the most important aspects of achieving on a higher level and not falling flat on your face.

A corporation that sells shoes can be imagined as a shoe store. The company is facing a challenger with state-of-the-art shoe technology that is gaining market share. Innovation, when implemented, might have its drawbacks. For example, if the first company is fearful of failure when using new methods and endeavours, it will not innovate and will become outdated quite quickly. If they welcome the chance of failure and go for it, they will develop new and exciting ideas until their previous products become trendy again.

Risk-taking, inventiveness, and the need to think beyond the box are encouraged by sprinting toward failure. It's worth considering failure while experimenting with fresh or unconventional ideas.

If you fear failing, then you won't achieve your full potential. Living your life imprisoned in a cage with only one small breathing hole is the result of allowing oneself to be frightened by the fear of failing.

You'll be upset when you find you have wasted the most important years of your life playing it safe.

Letting failure stop you from moving forward will mean that your life will only be as successful as your worst day.

Please also note that you seek inspiration and success from everyone you look to as a source of guidance and support. While their accomplishments are well-known, their failures before success aren't. Not all of them have managed to appear foolish, but they still are in the process of learning and getting better. Nevertheless, that has not hindered them. In other words, they have instead found out exactly what they need to know and have continued to grow and improve.

Henry Ford, the creator of Ford Motor Company, the maker of the first car widely available to the public, the Model T, had a successful career that lasted over fifty years.

Henry Ford started an unsuccessful automotive firm that competed with Thomas Edison's, the very first of its kind. The former manager was kicked out of his next job, which eventually leads to the creation of the Cadillac automobile firm. Having tarnished his name, he found a friend in Henry Ford, who formed the Ford Motor Company.

Ford was the first to implement modern assembly lines, which transformed factory procedures. He paid substantially above market value to keep the finest employees and was among the first to implement a 40-hour workweek.

Henry Ford was among the three richest men in the world when he began, but he ultimately failed each time he reached for great success.

You can learn from your mistakes, and failure doesn't negatively affect you. You aren't judged for failing, regardless of whether or not you succeed. People judge you if you resign and refuse to take responsibility for your errors.

There is no shame in getting up on your feet after being

knocked down. To gain something of value, you must be willing to take chances.

You're not defeated because you've been knocked down; you are defeated because you haven't gotten back up. You will always encounter obstacles. Regardless of setbacks, how you respond to risk is important.

It is a truth of life that failure is certain; what follows failure, however, has a huge influence on your character and the eventual amount of achievement. The good thing about failure is that it doesn't feel as horrible as it does the first time you encounter it.

16

The Surprising Power of Visualisation

EVEN THE TOP performers make mistakes. All the world's best athletes do it. There is a chance that your favourite actor or actress does it as well.

You've most likely done it on numerous occasions. Have you ever tried to remember where you've put your keys by shutting out everything else and visualising your house?

Visualisation is often under appreciated and often derided as being too much of a placebo.

Visualisation is more than just examining yourself in the mirror and thinking, "I'm the best in the world, so this is no problem!"

Visually rehearsing each step required to achieve a goal—every single minute step—is effective visualisation. Your mental pathways should be exercised first to increase your ability to recognise faults and discrepancies that you would otherwise make. It encourages you to use your critical thinking skills to focus on what you want to achieve and how.

Both seeing your achievement and having it impact your reality are intrinsically linked. When you adjust your concept of reality, you conceive more possibilities for yourself. Success is simply a perfect representation. Therefore, when you picture it, you are creating the proper framework for it.

It is important to be aware of every step from the beginning to the end, and everything in between, including final success.

When you view the details of every step, you will understand what stages you are missing, what more actions are required, and what shortcuts to explore.

More or less, visualisation enables you to examine the ideal pathway to accomplishment through creative and objective analysis. If you don't picture, you will be less able to think out of the box and consider new methods. Visualisation is a technique that gives you many options with no expense (or actual risk) save for the mental strain that it might entail.

On the face of it, this may seem like a difficult task, but believe it, it's nowhere like as difficult as beginning a process and having to change direction halfway through. Visualisation can be done while sleeping on a peaceful Saturday afternoon.

You can "wing it" if you visualise things. You'll only need to rehearse once if you see things as you want them to appear and imagine them regularly. Your second or third time through should result in a finished output.

Programming your brain to process and then recognise what is required for success happens due to the concentration and attention to detail that visualisation provides. You will have an easier time understanding and learning about little signs and be on high alert for things that will help you achieve your goals.

Many studies support this — the reticular activating system (RAS) within our brains enables us to be attentive to significant things.

When you envision, you have a huge role in selecting your RAS filters in what is remembered. This means that you notice things that will help you reach your goals, things you may have missed if you weren't looking for them.

In addition, visualising might help your task by breaking it down into smaller, manageable chunks. As daunting as it may be, when you look at tasks, a route to success, or a significant accomplishment, it's always best to think of them as achievable from the beginning. When there is only one large work you face, everything else may be an overwhelming challenge; yet, when all you face is a series of tasks, none of them is impossible.

When you divide your success down into many smaller milestones, it will encourage and boost your confidence. The difference between enthusiastically getting started on a task or hesitantly stepping into a task because you believe it will be a lot of work and painful.

There are two basic ways to prepare your mind to have success. Pretending you are sitting in a dark movie theatre and watching a movie in which you are the main character are both examples of the sensation known as "movie-viewing."

There are two movies, and you are doing one of two things:

The first movie has you going through every stage to complete something from a first-person perspective. Be aware of all the details, and do every task that's required. Sit in that scenario, feel it, and think about it. Preparing ahead of time for the stresses and curveballs ahead is a lot like rehearsing ahead of time.

When you view the second movie, you will do an action from a third-person perspective flawlessly. This helps you to concentrate on the details of your work and remember how satisfying it is when you accomplish it perfectly. You'll notice minor details you would have missed if you hadn't rehearsed it in advance. The penalty taker in football may practice repeatedly kicking the ball, noting each step, the direction he kicks, and the amount of force he puts behind his kicks.

Mental rehearsal positions your success as an inevitability.

COGNITIVE BENEFIT: There are numerous logical and common sense benefits of visualisation, and these benefits are backed by science.

According to French experts, it doesn't matter whether we're merely thinking about performing an action or are carrying it out in the real world. Although the brain isn't able to make the distinction, it's the same in both cases; thus, the same neural networks and connections are established and utilised. You're creating a trail of brain connections to be used when you need them.

It is implied that mental practice is just as physically demanding as physical practice. A study performed in 2007 concluded that mentally preparing for an exercise yielded strength improvements identical to performing the exercise physically.

One of the most overlooked and under utilised tools in business is visualisation.

17

Adjust Your Locus Of Control

A LOCUS of control describes where people believe that they have control in their life — whether this is inside or outside themselves. If you believe that external forces control your life, you have an external locus of control regardless of your efforts. In other words, the external locus view makes you little more than a passive observer, with virtually zero influence. In a sense, you may say that this is an extremely harmful mentality to your chances of success, happiness, and maximisation of your potential.

There is no rational way to be held responsible or to accept blame when you feel that you cannot exert any control. So you have no intention of ever-improving because you believe that your efforts have no relevance to your results.

Persons that dwell on past events are called "external locus" people. They are highly concentrated on situations in which they have no say. They spend their time helping others. They believe that individuals will miraculously change or that the issues that are affecting them would immediately stop. It is an act of desperation rather than hope or faith that drives them.

People focused on uncontrollable aspects of their lives have difficulty gaining a strong feeling of confidence and security. If they can't claim credit for their best successes, how can they develop their confidence? Their decisions will be driven by the circumstances in which they have little influence. The cycle continues to run itself.

Concern over issues you have no influence over is a waste of time. That opportunity may have been invested in activities that affect your income, standing in life, attractiveness, and health. We can boil it down to this: By sitting on your hands, you could have instead worked on certain activities that would have helped your life move forward. In contrast, you allow yourself to be dominated by a story that tells you that you have no control over your life. You cry yourself to sleep every night.

Rather than a person with an internal locus of control, let's compare them to someone with an external locus of control. The distinction between someone who believes that things happen due to their effort and ability and someone who believes that things happen because of outside factors and outside control is known as an internal locus of control vs. an external locus of control. If they fail, it's because they didn't work hard enough.

In contrast to those with an external locus of control, those with an internal locus of control feel that they are impacting the world instead of just being within it or subject to it. They're proactive because they believe the only way it will come to them is if they take the initiative.

As a result, they are focused on goals, as their decisions can affect whether or not their desires are fulfilled. They can have a huge impact on their lives every day.

By expectations, it's the folks with an internal locus of control who score highest on achievement.

WHAT's the difference in mindset between the two?

An internal locus individual will not accept a lack of success, and they are quick to work to change it. People who can only be influenced passively quietly accept whatever their circumstances dictate.

Here's an example to illustrate.

Inform others that you are often passed over for a promotion by less-experienced colleagues, especially younger workers. This is vexing, and this is where the centre of aggravation starts.

An outsider would likely assume that there's a plot underway. He believes that "My employer has always despised me. I threaten him because He also envies my wife." This is an example of an external locus of control since the discussed person blames outside factors instead of looking inward. They choose to be a victim.

To get back on track in the workplace, an internal locus person may begin scrutinising their actions and determining if these behaviours relate to their job performance. "Do I believe in it?" "Am I on time for work? Are eight hours a day enough? What do you mean by "minimum quality standards"? An example of departing early too regularly is taking overly long lunch breaks." They are focused on blaming themselves and not taking responsibility for their situation. To be a victor, one must choose to be.

That is very good news if the latter scenario sounds more similar to you. Since you understand that your activities cause your results, you will be more likely to have better results. What do you want to achieve? These belong to you, so grab them! Your ability to affect your life all begins and ends with your belief that when you concentrate on the things you can manage, you can completely change your life.

Not necessarily negative news is that the other situation sounds more familiar to you. It may not be on purpose. Your locus of control needs to be adjusted to include an awareness that your activities cause your results. Don't fret over things you cannot control; instead, use your energy to create change in your life. Don't bother making excuses!

Distinct people have different loci of control, which

doesn't affect how they think, feel, or act. What they go through is identical, yet they have different perceptions of it.

Results are the world's reward. There is no tolerance for excuses. It doesn't care about your original goal or your driving motivation. Regardless of the outcome, you are either a hero or a victim.

People who have internal loci of control accept reality as it is and make it happen the way they want. There is no blame placed on anyone or anything else when things go wrong. They take control and are accountable.

The view of the universe held by these individuals is that it consists of stimuli, all of which they have to respond to and take control of by exercising their will. Their main goal is to affect their immediate surroundings and maintain working in that area until their influence and control have expanded.

18

Your Decision-Making Method

THE SKILL of choosing decisions is not as simple as some may believe. You can't always pick the best answer from among the several possibilities out there since no one silver bullet question can help you each time you need it.

Do you want a hamburger or a taco?

This question has no long-term effects; thus, it's very easy to decide about. And even if you choose neither, you would still be just as content. Decisions are simple to make when they are on the east side.

While, of course, almost all of our choices have an impact that can last long after the decision has been made.

Is there a method we can produce consistently excellent decisions which will move us closer to realising our brand of success?

To sum it up, yeah. Decisions should be approached as a human being, where objective logic and emotive appeals are used to persuade.

Decisions are most often made devoid of human and emotional characteristics. However, this method is faulty because emotions speak to the happiness and mental well-being that decisions can bring. This is unacknowledged, though: that decisions can result in both emotional and mental well-being. It's essential. This has been demonstrated repeatedly; we are much more likely to be incorrect in forecasting our own emotions, and even if we're correct when forecasting our own, we are likely to be completely off the mark when it comes to forecasting the emotions of others.

The subjective part of making judgments should not be overlooked. Focusing solely on factual facts leads to frustration and failure. You may fail to discover important aspects of the decision if you attempt to simplify all of your major decisions to computation or a list of pros and cons.

For illustration, consider a woman who must decide between two marriage suitors.

He is perfect in every way. He comes from a well-off family; he has been to great schools and has always been incredibly generous.

The woman has a far better connection and feels incredible chemistry with the other suitor, but he doesn't have any of the attributes of the first suitor. But he is a good friend to her in many ways.

When cold logic was used, the choice would be made by the first suitor who possessed money and influence. Her entire life would be set up for her. She would never have to work again. Do you think she would be happier?

Thus, the most rational and reliable model for decision-making incorporates our human abilities and logic.

This decision-making process consists of four steps, and no one step deals only with subjective or objective viewpoints.

THE FOUR ELEMENTS that you must keep in mind are the context within which you are operating:

Emotions

It would help if you looked at how your decision affects you both personally and practically.

It must make you feel good and prevent making you feel bad. If it makes you happier in the short-term and long-term, it is successful. You expect that the positive feelings that you have right now will improve your mental well-being in the future.

At the second level, you must use your emotional resources to make decisions. What are your chances of succeeding when you base all of your decisions on sentiments of delight or rage and revenge?

The best decisions result from being rooted in one's emotions and understanding the emotional consequences of many options.

Self-identity

In a nutshell, you must know who you are and how you identify to make decisions.

If you allow your perceptions to match your actions, this is where you make your self-concept come true. Describe yourself honestly, and see if you can describe yourself as well as you'd like in the future.

How would you describe yourself? What are you constantly trying to convey when someone introduces you to a stranger?

It is crucial to realise that you are responsible for how you regard yourself. If you are consistent with it, you may remain happy and productive; however, if you are inconsistent, you can develop a state of cognitive dissonance.

Vision

The decisions you make in the long term will line up with your life goals and long-term vision.

When you have seen yourself in the future, this is how you see yourself. You are projecting yourself how you wish to appear for the next five years. Are you now closer to achieving your goal, or are you farther away?

This refers to your identity, but it has more to do with your social standing than your inherent qualities.

Context

Your finest decisions will stem from you living in, being from, and striving to enter a certain setting.

You can't keep making the same decision under new circumstances. Be aware of the things and people around you, and notice how they shape your emotions, self-identity, and visions. Unfortunately, our judgments can't be made in a vacuum, and their ramifications for others must be considered. You must understand all of the variables, and then you must decide how to balance your personal preferences and how your actions may affect others.

This is why following a formula in your decision-making is impossible. Let's have a look at how these four aspects may influence a decision.

If you are deciding whether to remain at your current job or accept a job you have been offered by another company, pretend like you are considering this decision.

Instead of solely considering how much higher your salary or how much you like your current co-workers, you need to engage in a holistic and human decision-making process.

IN SUMMARY:

EMOTIONAL: Do you feel you are deciding from positive or negative motivation, for example, to spite your current superintendent? Do you get excited thinking about the new role, and do you have a positive outlook on your career as a result?

Self-identity: Do you like the new role and view yourself as that person? Are you talented, have fun doing it, and can learn and grow? What would you do if you told your friends about your new job?

Vision: Is it getting you closer to your personal and professional goals, such as increasing your income or better balancing your work and personal lives? Do you believe that this job and your values are a good match?

Context: How will this role affect the people with whom you work? Is it going to harm or strengthen the relationships you need for the future? Is the new company heading in the right direction, or has it started to sink?

19

The Value Of Ignoring

REGARDLESS OF WHETHER or not you have catalogued your ideas, everyone has some notion of what they must do. As you may expect, establish a to-do list to help you remember everything.

While this chapter focuses on things you should avoid, here are some do's and don'ts to keep in mind while writing your to-do list.

Then, the night before, write a to-do list. Do this so you can get right into the middle of things the next day, just when you open your eyes. Making your daily to-do list first thing in the morning causes you to rush, resulting in unclear priorities. The project is much clearer when you work on it the night before. This enables you to think more clearly about what you have to do in the following days, weeks, and months. This is a technique that will go a long way toward helping you.

Additionally, you should only add three to five activities to your to-do list. On the other hand, this can seem like a small number, but it helps you zero in on the most important goals you've planned for the day. You can also schedule your weekly and monthly duties correctly, avoiding overburden one day and neglecting the next. You will learn more about your priorities as well.

Additionally, consider which chores you want to do each day, as well as how ambitious you want to be. Identifying three to five difficult tasks or projects you detest will do nothing to help you complete the challenging tasks. Look for easy, challenging, despised, and delightful chores to mix things up. That way, you will not hate getting out of bed in the morning. Warming up is easy because you may do it and lead to your daily duties simultaneously. To be successful, you must have momentum and be mindful of your inertia, which can be toxic.

For the final time, disregard everything else! Clear the area in front of you so you may chop the wood. Rather than chasing the latest trends, work on achieving your best every day. The first step is to know what you must do, but it is equally as important to recognise what you should not be doing.

On the other hand, create a "do not" list alongside your "do" list. Use these instructions to prepare to chop the tree in front of you. In other words, it will help you identify your priorities and get you prepared for success.

HERE's what you should put on your don't-do list.

The first item on the list is important duties but are out of your control at the moment.

External factors make these activities impossible. They may be waiting for input from others, or they could need more time to progress or develop. Mark these items as things you will never be able to control because there is absolutely nothing you can do about them. It's a complete waste of time because you're dedicating your mental capacity to them. When other elements are in place, you may focus on these other tasks.

A third thing to avoid is duties that you shouldn't be doing or jobs that you should delegate. You will have to think critically about your assignments and cut anything that is not necessary.

You should identify all jobs that are unique to you and identify all tasks that can be done equally or even better by others. Often, this is work that you don't want to do, such as the type of work you might perform if you have no other choice. Is it possible to assign them elsewhere, or can they be outsourced? There are larger activities that only you can accomplish and minor, repetitive tasks that you shouldn't waste time on.

Next, jobs that are adequate but do not require significant extra effort. Most of them are tasks. Any more effort doesn't improve most activities, and if they are, the effect is minimal and negligible.

Work that suffers from large diminishing returns includes a lot of these activities. This assignment still has plenty of room for improvement, but on the other hand, this task has fulfilled its aim. Try to avoid wasting your time on them, and don't allow yourself to fall into the trap of considering these things as a high priority. For example, is your sock drawer that messy, or is it as messy as it needs to be to serve its primary function and purpose? Is having well-organised socks going to assist you in your life?

One of the primary reasons we can't fully focus on our genuine priorities is because we're afraid we missed anything. However, no matter how well you plan, you cannot account for everything, so prioritising is best.

You can use the to-do list for this. Once you've considered everything and you have determined that everything on your "not to do" list isn't relevant, you should presumably be able to concentrate without stress.

A cluttered mind will increase stress and worry, and the fewer things that occupy your thoughts, the better. Both stress and worry reduce one's chances of achievement.

Chopping the wood in front of you frees your mind from

the load of having too many things in the air. This eliminates most of the objects in the air, helping you to focus on what is in front of you. You can focus on the wood in front of your axe and dispatch multiple pieces of wood in rapid succession.

20

The Perfectionism Devil

PERFECTIONISM IS ALSO KNOWN as fear of failure.

Criticism directed at yourself is self-deprecating and self-destructive.

To succeed, you must defeat your perfectionist instincts.

The assumption that "perfection is necessary" is mistaken.

The image you have of the world and what people expect is unrealistic. The operation room and the courtroom are expected to be immaculate, but imperfection is part of everyday life elsewhere.

Nobody is ever in a position to condemn you because everyone understands that they've made mistakes in their own lives. This happens to everyone occasionally.

Everyone is flawed, even celebrities like Kate Upton and Hugh Jackman. Expectations for perfection from others mean that you're not going to get it. Expectations for perfection from others mean that you won't receive it. From a logical perspective, since there is no such thing as a flawless individual, we cannot expect others to be perfect.

To be successful, you must realise that people accept imperfection. Everything we do has varying shades of grey, and in the rest of the world, people rarely act with black and white absolutes.

When you aren't required to spend time painstakingly getting things right, you have the freedom to move forward and tackle the difficulties standing in your way. You have to be perfect to finish something, which means that if any detail is not correct, you will never be done (in your view). A more accurate statement is that you only produce or capture a very small percentage of your true potential. Sometimes, this tiny percentage is useless on its own and hence does not satisfy your overall objectives.

The search for perfection slows you down. Moving at a snail's pace will be your lot in life if you constantly keep glancing back and verifying your handiwork. at best, you can achieve a small percentage of what you intended; otherwise, you're trapped in analytical paralysis and have nothing to show for it

Of course, minimum standards exist.

For your goals to be attained and success obtained, your performance must be of a specific level of competence.

However, examining costs and benefits is necessary to determine the ideal association between perfectionism and productivity.

Also, what degree of specificity is needed to support your supervisor?" Your boss will probably never see the report if you strive for a very in-depth level of detail. If you don't give the job your full attention, you may end up with something of little value. To accomplish these goals, what amount of perfectionism would the report allow and include?

The identical thing that ruins momentum also holds people back from their goals, which should be utilised daily.

In order to break the inertia of any work, you must put in considerable effort. If you're stuck in the grip of perfectionism, you've derailed and will have to exert a huge amount of effort to pick things up again.

Have you ever just been "in the zone?" That's momentum, and that's almost certainly a result of letting go of perfectionism. It's when thoughts just come to you, and you're not thinking about it; you're just performing. It doesn't matter if things don't turn out perfectly because all you have to do is just continue to translate your thoughts into words or work.

For this particular definition, perfectionism is also known as procrastination because it gives you an excuse to delay future steps.

Focusing on maximising production and the larger picture is the fundamental problem with perfectionists. They lose sight of the forest because they're too absorbed in the trees. They should be striving for the larger aim of the forest instead. Think of it this way: Once you've reached perfection, there will be diminishing returns; nevertheless, the big picture goal will still be there, waiting for you.

The Pareto Principle is a useful concept for you to embrace to defeat perfectionism.

For background, the land in Italy was split into two nearly equal parts in 1906, with 20% of the population owning 80% of the land.

Everything about human life can be mapped according to the Pareto principle, including work, relationships, and career, among other things. Taking use of the Pareto Principle will help you maximise your time.

80% of the results you hope to obtain from a task will be accomplished by the work done by 20% of your time and energy dedicated to it.

I.e., the vast majority of your results are determined by the 20% of your everyday duties that account for most of your results. In other words, 80% of your effort is concentrated on getting the job done perfectly, while the other 20% is ensuring that the job is complete.

80% of your revenue is generated by the 20% of your activities that you are doing in any given month, whereas the extra effort you put in beyond 20% has an increasingly negligible effect. You will often obtain "good to great" results with only 20% of the effort. When it comes to "getting too awesome/perfect," the effort and money aren't worth it. And, most importantly, spending so much time and money isn't worth the anguish it produces in virtually every case.

It would be best if you learned to know when 80% of your work is required and whether or not it is worth it.

Failing to recognise this trend means you will be stuck on 80% of the effort that doesn't significantly influence your bottom line. Once your productivity and output are reduced, your results will decrease.

The second technique of avoiding perfectionism might be considered as applying this idea. Once you know that it's impossible to gain any more benefit from working on something, you may maximise your success. Similar to this stage is where the aim of the assignment is completely satisfied and where people don't notice any further work or attention to detail.

This is something that many creatives don't realise. Success is never about the intentions or how flawless something is. It's all about getting outcomes. One of the most critical realisations along the road to success is that you can defeat your perfectionist demon.

Focus on the Journey

A lot of people fail to grasp that the modest steps, the missteps, and the rough patches that must be overcome are what they want. Individuals want to benefit from their experiences, and journeys have a lot more to give than any destination. Often our idea of success (the destination) changes along the way.

While this analogy is true, your entire life is not just a journey; it is a gradual journey towards death. In that case, why travel to the end if all the nice stuff occurs along the way?

There is a long journey to success. The view is that it is a gruelling road with ups and downs, followed by a happy outcome. Whether or not that is the case, it is really important to pause occasionally and appreciate the small things in life.

Alternatively, success is more readily achieved by concentrating on the journey rather than on the destination.

Staring just at the destination puts blinders on and blocks out everything that doesn't serve the plan for achievement.

Since goals often change based on new information, this can be exceedingly detrimental. When new knowledge reveals the new goals to be unrealistic or detrimental, we have to reconsider our initial intentions. When you can concentrate on the overall path, you will be free to make the kinds of changes that prevent you from having a total stall. If you focus too much on the goal, you'll miss out on valuable lessons about the journey.

Let's say Jackson (who is now without a car) has completely dedicated himself to creating an engine for a 1969 Corvette that will fit in the frame. That certainly is a lovely vehicle. He didn't care about how he got there as long as he arrived. However, while on his trip, Jackson had to obtain a wife and a child, and he realised that rebuilding a Ford 150 would be faster and cheaper. A nice vehicle to look at.

Even if the new circumstances in his life have changed Jackson's ultimate destination, would it be the same? If you can only afford and plan to use a sports car for yourself, is it still prudent to buy one? Since this is the case, his new destination will only be a car for his family that is completely secure.

By focusing on the journey, you uncover new goals and definitions of success that you may not have previously discovered. Your personal development and your overall enjoyment of life will be impeded if you don't give your current experiences the attention they deserve.

You miss out on an opportunity if you aren't in the moment. Since you're too goal-oriented ever to make a detour or use back lanes, you will never be able to veer off course. It is more likely to occur on backstreets, though, as backstreets tend to lead to shortcuts, new developments, and other types of success altogether. Perhaps more than anything, unexpected backstreets provide you with the most memorable experiences of your life. Whereas, with a goal-orientated approach, conventional logic may have ignored them. Rigidity is the other route to another person's concept of success rather than yours.

Another benefit of looking at a long-term perspective is that it teaches you the virtue of delayed gratification and patience, as it is a realistic approach. Results in the short term (or even any results) are extremely rare. To reduce your tension and concern about succeeding and accomplishing goals, set low expectations for yourself, but focus on the present now and chop wood.

Delayed gratification is a major obstacle to long-term success for impulsive persons and requires an instant reward. They believe their achievement is only possible if it's achieved quickly and simpler.

Delayed gratification has long been shown to be a powerful attribute, and it's substantially connected with success. At that moment, two pieces of candy were offered to those who waited. In follow-up studies, the children who made the choice that was later rated as better had higher levels of competence as well as higher test scores.

To sum it up, destination-oriented activities are always on the rise. You'll be left wanting more after you reach your destination. The experience and knowledge you gain during your trip will overshadow the final destination.

Success will depend on whether you stay focused on the journey. If you focus on the journey, there is no worst-case scenario. No matter where you start or what road you take, you'll always be acquiring new knowledge and gaining new experiences, making it a total no-brainer to follow your path to success. When you are focused on your destination, there is no question whether you have succeeded or failed. Reaching the destination is not even a worst-case scenario.

Ultimately, it is up to you to discover that the trip is more important than the destination. While you are present, make the most of each moment you have.

Afterword

There is just one direct, indisputable reason for remaining in our comfort zone, never attempting to step beyond our established boundaries, and never obtaining what we want—**fear.**

To progress, we must remove the obstacles of fear and blockages of energy that stand in our way. We must be exceptional at identifying our concerns and how they compound to hold us back and must be able to release these anxieties to keep moving forward.

When all memories and experiences are transformed into wisdom, we may become ourselves completely, without any restrictions. This places us in a position to carry ourselves forward, even if it is really difficult. We can face anything when we reach this stage of our lives and no longer doubt the course of life.

The thing to remember is that we're all tougher than we realise since we can manage whatever comes our way. So, it doesn't matter. Accepting and learning to trust in oneself are important.

When you permit yourself to open new doors, the universe gives you all the support you need and grants you access to an unending supply of opportunities.

Never lose faith in yourself and know that no matter what

may occur on your journey, you're on the right route, leading you to where you want to be and where you expect to be.

Our desire for you is to allow you to have infinite possibilities to be in contact with Mother Nature's majestic magnificence, spiritual sanctuaries like libraries, museums, and gurdwaras, and to connect with other people from all walks of life.

On your road to uncovering all of this wealth, you will eventually identify yourself as the person you believe you were born to be. You must establish and maintain healthy self-relationships. You can't truly love others unless you learn and accept who you are.

Become your own hero. Rise and lead the self-possessed life you have created for yourself. The best way to do this is to ignore the many competing voices from the crowd shouting for attention and focus on your voice. If you are afraid of success, don't worry—you won't succeed. Realise your desires and fulfil them. Don't be afraid to achieve great things. Listen to your heart and make good on its longings.

The world is waiting just for you.

Feedback

Thank you for reading 'How To Say Goodbye To Your Comfort Zone'. We hope you enjoyed the book? If you have a free moment, please leave us some feedback on Amazon.

Also, scan the QR code below to visit our website where you can find more information on our range of books available.

HackneyandJones.com

www.ingramcontent.com/pod-product-compliance
Lightning Source LLC
Chambersburg PA
CBHW031545080526
44588CB00018B/2708